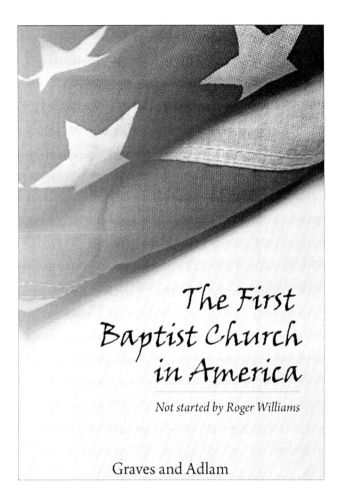

The First
Baptist Church
in America

Not started by Roger Williams

Graves and Adlam

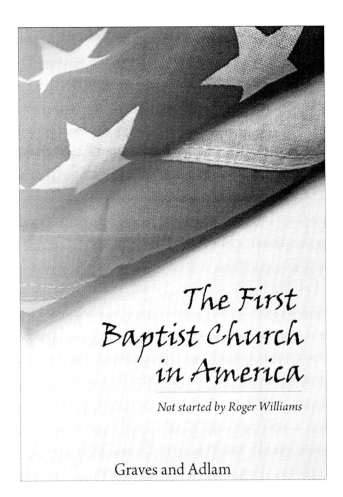

The First Baptist Church in America

Not started by Roger Williams

Graves and Adlam

Reprinted 2010 by Calvary Publishing
A Ministry of Parker Memorial Baptist Church
1902 East Cavanaugh Road
Lansing, Michigan 48910
www.CalvaryPublishing.org

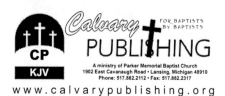

DEDICATED

To

The Three Millions of American Baptists

Whose unflinching loyalty to "the Truth"

As it is in Jesus

And for Jesus,

Has ever been their proud boast;

Who we believe will accept

Historical Facts

In preference to

Historical Misapprehensions and

Inherited Partialities;

In justice to the memory of a fellow-witness whose

Name and fame

Have been for centuries shaded and unhonored,

This Vindication is

Confidently dedicated

By its Author and Editor.

TABLE OF CONTENTS

PART I.

PART II.

He seized the whip, and laid on the blows in an
unmerciful manner.

Part First

INTRODUCTION.

BY THE EDITOR.

IF any apology is needed for presenting this refutation of what is claimed for Roger Williams and the First Baptist Church, of Providence, R. I., in disparagement of the just claims of Dr. John Clarke and the First Baptist Church, of Providence, R. I., it must be found,

First — In the claims of exact historical truths, as opposed to historical misapprehensions and inherited fancies and partialities.

Second — The more particular and personal reasons that compelled me to interest myself in these investigations, and to give their results to the public, is the fact that in the many public discussions with Pedobaptists and Campbellite opponents, in which the origin and histories of our respective denominations have been a prominent subject, they have constantly and defiantly asserted that, granting our own principles, Baptists are without either baptism, ordinances, or even a *history* that entitles them to be considered churches of Christ, having been originated, but a few years since, by one Roger Williams, a Pedobaptist, who virtually baptized himself and eleven other Pedobaptists, and organized them into a Baptist Church, the first one in America, and for years was its pastor, transmitting his invalid baptism to all succeeding Baptist Churches in America; and, therefore, if it is true that "without baptism there can be no church,"—a truth admitted by all ecclesiastical writers. Baptist organizations are not churches of Christ, and can not be

(11)

considered the visible constituents and executors of His kingdom.

Third—Another and final reason: It is unquestionably a duty we owe to Christ and to ourselves, as the professed representatives of His churches, to vindicate our history from every charge that is calculated to disparage or prejudice it in the estimation of men. It is but loyalty to our Savior and King to do this.

Not for a moment believing that the Baptist Churches in America, or even the First Baptist Church at Providence, R. I., had such an indefensible origin—which unbelief was confirmed by an historical Book, by Dr. Adlam, seen some years before, challenging the claims of the Providence church to the honor of being the first church in America, I resolved, in the year 1854-5, to visit the contending churches to learn all it was possible to be gathered from personal intercourse and observation.

On reaching Newport, R. I., I became acquainted with Dr. S. Adlam, the historian of Rhode Island, and pastor of the First Baptist Church of the city, in whose historical information and integrity all men of the island had the most unbounded confidence. From him I learned that he had embodied in that Book (above referred to) all his historical authorities, by which he claimed he had conclusively established the prior claims of Newport over the Providence church, and that, in the near future, he should accede to the request of " The Newport Historical Society " to deliver an "Historical Address," discussing the question of the authorship of the charter of 1663, which would contain a large amount of valuable and hitherto unpublished historical information.*

* This Address will be found in Part III. This information rendered a long, tedious personal investigation of the documents unnecessary. Under the guidance of Bro. Adlam I sought the neglected grave of Dr. John Clarke, and digging away a mould, which had accumulated at the foot of his tombstone, I read as follows:

To the Memory of
DOCTOR JOHN CLARKE,
*One of the original purchasers and proprietors of
this island and one of the founders of the
First Baptist Church of Newport,
its first pastor and munificent benefactor;
He was a native of Bedfordshire, England,
and a practitioner of physic in London.
He, with his associates, came to this island from Mass.,
in March, 1638, O. S., and on the 24th
of the same month obtained a deed thereof from
the Indians. He shortly after gathered
the church aforesaid and became its pastor.
In 1651, he, with Roger Williams. was sent to England,
by the people of Rhode Island Colony,
to negotiate the business of the Colony with the
British ministry. Mr. Clarke was instrumental
in obtaining the Charter of 1663 from Charles II., which
secured to the people of the State free and
full enjoyment of judgment and conscience in matters
of religion. He remained in England
to watch over the interests of the Colony until 1664,
and then returned to Newport and
resumed the pastoral care of his church.
Mr. Clarke and Mr. Williams, two fathers of the Colony,
strenuously and fearlessly maintained that
none but Jesus Christ had authority
over the affairs of conscience. He died
April 20, 1676, in the 66th year
of his age, and is here interred.*

I sat for hours before this silent witness, sending busy recollections—of recorded events—back over the fancied scenes and transactions of the two centuries past, when these sturdy witnesses of Christ, fleeing from the persecutions of the Old World, found, in their wanderings, this haven, and cleared away the dense wilderness, and let in, for the first time, God's glorious sunlight upon this beautiful island, by the "loud resounding sea." and thanked their God for it, as their peaceful home that seemed to them but a recovered part of Paradise itself.

It occurred to me that the testimony of monuments erected at, or very near, the time of the events commemorated, and by those personally conversant or *best* conversant with them, are the most reliable witnesses of the events recorded.

Written records—histories—are seldom made until years, and often many years after the events recorded, and are largely dependent upon reports and the treacherous memories of interested parties.

Mural witnesses never forget. Written records are often lost, and mistakes, especially of dates, are very liable to occur in the most painstaking attempts to reproduce them.

A mural record is never lost so long as the enduring marble remains.

This monument was doubtless erected by the very hands that laid the loved and honored dead to rest in this lovely spot.

Dr. Clarke left no child or relative to contribute this then costly mark of affection. The worn appearance of the stone testifies to its extreme age, and the language and style of the epitaph witness that it has come down to us from "former generations"—the centuries past.

I unhesitatingly accepted this mural witness as unimpeachable, and studied it, examining and cross-examining it for the utmost syllable of its testimony.

From it I learned,

First—That John Clarke was one of the first founders of the First Baptist Church, of Newport, R. I.

Second—That the First Baptist Church, of Newport, R. I., was unquestionably founded in

1638.

Third—That Dr. John Clarke was undoubtedly its first pastor, and continued to be so until the day of his death.

Fourth—That this church has had a continuous existence from "1638" until the present.

Fifth—That this date (corresponding as it did with the testimony of Governor Winthrop and that given by Crosby, the eminent English historian, and both confirmed by the foot-note on the 453d page of "The History of the Philadelphia Association," published by the American Baptist Publication Society, and Backus' "History of New England Baptists," which were familiar to me), I was here compelled to decide correct, unless it could be unquestionably proved that the 1638 upon this monument is fictitious, and by fourteen years too early, or that the First Church in Providence, R. I., was constituted prior to 1638, and had had a continued existence from that time until the present.

Sixth—That the First Church at Newport, and not the First Church at Providence, is the First Baptist Church in America, and that Dr. John Clarke, and not Roger Williams, was the founder and pastor of the First Baptist Church in Rhode Island and America.

This was the very question I had come to Rhode Island to solve.

But I read on, surprised at the confirmation of another honor claimed for Dr. Clarke by his friends, but attributed to Roger Williams by historians, through the influence of his relatives and the Baptists of Providence, viz:

Seventh—" That Mr. Clarke was instrumental in obtaining the Charter of 1663 from Charles II., which secured to the people of the State free and full enjoyment of conscience and judgment in matters of religion, etc."

I particularly noticed the language—it was John Clarke alone, and not John Clarke and, or in connection with Roger Williams, who procured from Charles II. the Charter of 1663.*

With these "facts and figures" in hand I hurried on to Providence to obtain the *ipissima verba* of its claims, as inscribed upon the Tablet placed upon the walls of its audience room, which I found to be as follows:

---

* The claims of Dr. Clarke will fbe fully discussed and settled in Dr. Adlam's Historical Address, which concludes this work.

> "*This Church was founded in* 1639, *by Rodger Williams, its first pastor, and the first Asserter of Liberty of Conscience.*
> *It was the*
> *First Church in Rhode Island and the First Baptist Church in America.*"

At the first reading. only one statement fixed my vision, as though it were the only statement on the Tablet, and filled me with unmeasured astonishment! It was the third line, "the first Asserter of liberty of conscience." It is an unqualified assertion, limiting it to no age or nation!! This is attributing to one man, in the seventeenth century, the glory and honor belonging to Christ alone, and for re-assertion and vindication of which the apostles and more than ten millions of His witnesses laid down their lives.

The Great Teacher of Galilee was the First Asserter of Liberty of Conscience.

Christ, the Supreme Lawgiver in all things pertaining to His worship, is the chief corner stone on which He built His Church and Kingdom.

" On this rock [The Christ] will I build my church ; and the gates of Hades shall not prevail against it."—Matt. xvi. 18.

Mark His most emphatic law of obedience:

"Call no *man master;* for *one* is your Master, even Christ ; and all ye are brethren."—Matt. xxiii. 8.

2

This explicitly forbids His disciples, in all ages and nations, to recognize the right of any one to dictate to them in matters of religious faith or practice, for only One in heaven or on earth possesses that right, and he is our Christly Lord.

Again:

" Neither be ye called masters: for one is your Master, even Christ the anointed King of Zion, and all ye are brethren."

This is a positive command that His disciples—no one who recognizes Him as Lord—should presume to usurp, or by yielding obedience thereto, favor the usurpation of authority dictated in matters pertaining to His worship.

And again:

" Render therefore unto Cæsar the things which are Cæsar's · and unto God the things that are God's.—Matt. xxii. 21.

The best comment on this passage is in the petition of the Anabaptists, presented to James I. in 1620:

" The vileness of persecuting the body of any man only for the cause of conscience, is against the Word of God and law of Christ."

Again:

"Oh! be pleased to consider why you should persecute us for humbly beseeching you in the words of the King of kings to give unto God the things which are God's, which is to be Lord and Lawgiver to the soul in that spiritual worship and service which He requireth. If you will take away this from God, what is it that is

God's ? Far be it from you to sit in the consciences of men to be lawgiver and judge therein, This is anti-christ's practice persuading the kings of the earth to give him their power to compel all hereunto."*

It was the soul-liberty, inspired by this law of Christ, that enabled Peter and John to stand forth before the rulers of the Jews, whom they had commanded, on pain of punishment, not to speak at all, nor teach in the name of Jesus, and answer them :

"Whether it be right in the sight of God to hearken unto you more than unto God, judge ye."—Acts iv. 19.

Leanord Busher, a citizen of London, and a Baptist, as early as 1614, presented to James I. and to Parliament his "Religious Peace; or, Plea for Liberty of Conscience;" published it in pamphlet form, which Dr. Cathcart pronounces one of the most remarkable productions ever printed.†

---

*An humble supplication to the King's Majesty.

†" Among the notes of the early English Baptists, mention must not be omitted of the fact that to one of their number belongs the honor of having produced the first work in our language in advocacy of religious liberty. In 1614 appeared a tract entitled, 'Religion's Peace; or, A Plea for Liberty of Conscience.' Its author was Leonard Busher. He spoke for Baptists then and evermore. Not once in all their history have they violated the principles of Busher's plea. Bancroft is slightly in error when he says of Roger Williams (Vol. I., 375), that ' he was the first person in modern Chris-tendom to assert in its plentitude the doctrine of the liberty of conscience, the equality of opinions before the law.' Busher was more than twenty years in advance of Williams with the same doctrine in all its fullness. But the great historian is indisputably correct when he says : 'Freedom of conscienee, unlimited freedom of mind, was from the first the trophy of the Baptists.'" (Vol. II., 67.)

This work was followed by another treatise on the same subject, and published in 1615, "by Christ's unworthy witnesses, His Majesty's faithful subjects, commonly, but unjustly, called Anabaptists."

Still another treatise followed in 1620, with these pleas and published treatises. Roger Williams was familiar long before he left England, and by them the fires of soul liberty were kindled upon the altar of his heart.

With such evident misapprehension and misstatements of historical facts before my eyes, I confess my faith in the information and reliability of the author was severely shaken:

I read again:

> "*This Church*
> *was founded in* 1639."

A new light broke in upon my mind, making me wonder I had not seen it before—founded in 1639!! Granting the dates of constitution claimed by each contesting church to be correct, then it is undeniably true that

The Newport Church is the Elder by One Full Year.

This fact forever settles the question as to which of these churches is the First Baptist Church in Rhode Island and the First Baptist Church in America.

It is the First Church in Newport, and Not the First Church in Providence, R. I.

The next source of information sought was the venerable Dr. David Benedict, who resided at Pawtucket, R. I.—the Historian of American Baptists.

Upon giving my name I was kindly welcomed as the "Author of the Great Iron Wheel." I found him hard at work on his "History of the Donatists," translating his authorities out of Latin. (The notes of that interview being lost the following can be relied upon as his sentiments.) Touching the conflicting claims of the Newport and Providence churches above referred to, and his verdict in favor of Providence, expressed in his History, he remarked, that "it was his rule not to go behind the records of the churches. His verdict was in accordance with the records of the Providence church. If he had erred he had been misled by those records, and with no intention to disparage the claims of the Newport church. He admitted the growing perplexities that had for years confused and unsettled his mind as to the correctness of Mr. James Stanford's history of the Providence church, *compiled without any church record*, and a full century after its origin. It would not be strange, but indeed probable, that errors, and not a few, would occur." Alluding to the treatment of our brethern, at Newport, by the Pedobaptists of Massachusetts: "There was not much affiliation or pulpit communion in Boston when a Pedobaptist sheriff forced Brethren Clarke and Holmes into their meeting-house, and Brother Clarke protested

by 'sitting with his hat on.'" Ah, times have won-
derfully changed. Then Pedobaptists scourged and
imprisoned our people as not fit to live in the land,
and now they persecute us from their pulpits and
presses because we won't commune with them! Won-
derful change!*

As the sun was setting, he remarked, "Would you
not like to take a little walk with me, for exercise?
It is time for me to get up the cow, and you must stay
and take tea with me." To this I readily assented.
A short walk to the edge of the village brought us to
the pasture bars where old Dolly waited for her master—and a nice animal she was. We followed her to
the cow-pen, and I saw the old patriarch dexterously
draw forth a booming pail of creamy milk. When
called into "tea" there was a clean spread and a bowl
of *milk*, a plate of nice light bread, and a small roll of
yellow butter, and a saucer of delicious red currants,
fresh from the bush, beside each plate. It was a nice
"tea," with the tea left out. I mention these things to
show the reader Dr. B's simple mode of living, which
was the secret of his hale and vigorous constitution at
ninety. We thought of Goldsmith's village parson:

"Passing rich, with forty pounds a year."

---

* Dr. Benedict, in his "Fifty Years Among the Baptists," says: "At that
time the exchange of pulpits between the advocates and the opponents of
infant baptism was of very rare occurrence, *except in a few of the more distinguished churches in the Northern States*. Indeed the doctrine of non-
intercourse, so far as ministerial services were concerned, almost universally prevailed between Baptists and Pedobaptists," pp. 94, 95.

This was an old Baptist landmark, surely.

Another question discussed: " Are the Church Records of the First Baptist Church, of Providence. R. I., Reliable? If so, what follows?

With these "facts and figures" gathered on the ground, I returned home awakened to other inquiries, viz: Are the church records of the First Baptist Church, of Providence, R. I., and the statements on that Tablet reliable? and if so, what conclusions effecting the fundamental principles of our church polity follow?

The statements are, that that church was organized in 1639, and is the successor of that society, or "thing called a church," which Roger Williams gathered and immersed, and of which he was for years pastor, and succeeded by Mr. Onley, whom he immersed, and thus his irregular baptism (?) was transmitted to the Baptist Churches of New England, and onward. If these facts are granted, and those immersions admitted to be scriptural and valid baptisms, then it follows :

First—That an *unbaptized* man, and not even a *member*, and much less an officer of any church of Christ, can administer valid baptism, and to whom and where ever he pleases; and,

Second—That a company of persons so immersed, and that without any profession of personal regeneration, and without "creed or covenant," or shadow of scriptural organization, is, and should be considered, a veritable Church of Christ, and clothed with all ecclesiastical authority.

And these statements admitted, it unanswerably follows:

Third—What all our ecclesiastical opposers charge is true, viz: That the First Baptist Church of America— and very naturally concluded—the Baptist denomination, was originated but a little over two hundred years ago by Roger Williams, an unbaptized and *excluded Pedobaptist*, who was virtually himself a se-Baptist, or se-immersionist, he having been immersed by another unbaptized and excluded Pedobaptist. These acts Baptists, as well as all others, admit were not Christian baptisms, but "null and void," and, therefore, no American Baptist can tell whether he is baptized or not, or whether there is a scripturally organized Baptist Church in America, since, as all ecclesiastical writers admit, without a scriptural baptism there can be no church.* It is not strange that Dr. Caldwell (for several years the pastor of the First Church in Providence), should say of Williams' company, called a *church*, "It was a novel; elsewhere it might have seemed *revolutionary*,"†

He could have as truly said, it should *everywhere* seem revolutionary, because evidently subversive of every principle of church building and polity recognized by Baptists.

That the immersions of unbaptized, *i. e.*, unimmersed, or illegally immersed and unordained men, were by American Baptists considered revolutionary, I sub-

---

* Rev. N. L. Rice (Presbyterian) in his work on "Baptism."

† See his two hundred and fiftieth Historical Address, delivered April 28, 1889.

mit the repeated decisions of the Philadelphia Baptist
Association from the year 1707–1807.

"In the year 1732 a question was moved whether
a person, not being baptized himself, and presuming
in private [*i. e.*, without the knowledge or consent of
a church] to baptize another, whether such pretended
baptism be valid or no, or whether it might not be
adjudged a nullity?"

Resolved, We judge such baptism, as invalid and no
better than if it had never been done.*

This was the case of Roger Williams' own baptism,
and those he administered to the company he immersed and formed into the First Baptist Church, of
Providence, according to its records. If there can be
no such church without baptism, that body is not and
never was a church.

In 1744 we find this query and answer:

"Suppose a person, baptized by a man, who takes
upon himself to preach the gospel, and proceeds to
administer the ordinances without a regular call or
ordination from any chuch, whether the person so
baptized may be admitted into any orderly church—
yea or nay?"

Resolved, We can not encourage such irregular proceedings, because it hath ill-consequences every way
attending it; it is also opposite to our discipline [*i. e.*,
"revolutionary"]. We, therefore, give our sentiments
that such administrations are irregular, invalid and
of no effect.

Was not this Roger William's baptism? Was he
not immersed by a man who was not only himself

---

* Minutes Philadelphia Baptist Association, p. 33.

unbaptized, unordained, but a member of no church, and was not his own baptism invalid and of no effect? Was not Roger Williams' immersions, as well as Holliman's *null* himself, being both unbaptized and unordained? If, therefore, the statements of the Providence church are true, that church (?) never was and is not a church. But I rejoice in being able to prove that its Church Records are not true. Roger Williams did not found it, and was never the pastor of it, and never baptized any member into it.

In 1768, "in answer to a query from New York, it was agreed that baptism administered by a person not ordained, was *invalid and disorderly,*" (p. 104.)

Was not both Holliman and Roger Williams unordained, and were not their so-called baptisms invalid and disorderly? And if the Providence Church Records are correct, has that church the shadow of a claim to be a church of Christ, and have not her ordinances since 1639 been both *invalid and disorderly*? "Can a clean thing come out of an unclean?" Can valid and orderly ordinances come from invalid and disorderly ones? Time can not bring something out of nothing—*ex nihilo nihil fit*. But I rejoice to be able, by authentic documents, to prove that they are not correct, and to indicate the claims of the Providence church to being a scriptural church to-day, and that she has been so from the day of her constitution in 1652.

In 1792 "a query respecting the validity of baptism administered by an unordained and unbaptized admin-

istrator * was taken up and **determined in the nega-
tive.''**

Was not Ezekiel Holliman, who immersed Roger
Williams, both unordained and unbaptized?

Was not Roger Williams, who immersed all the
members of the First Baptist Church in 1639, both
unordained and unbaptized? If his administration
was both invalid and disorderly, was that company,
so immersed (?), baptized, or in any sense a church at
all? Certainly not. It was worse than a "novel"—
it was revolutionary—and all the proceedings connected with it subversive of every principle of Baptist
Church polity, according to the judgment of the Philadelphia Baptist Association, which, in 1708, embraced
all the Baptist churches in America.

Dr. Caldwell said, and doubtless with an intended
slight, that the proceedings of Roger Williams in organ-

* In the minutes of the Elkhorn Association, for the year 1822, we find
the following:

"The committee, to whom the following queries from the First Baptist
Church. of Lexington, were referred, viz: 1. Can persons baptized on a
profession of faith, by an administrator not regularly ordained, be received
into our churches under any circumstances whatever. without being again
baptized?

"Report in answer to the first query, that it is not regular to receive
such members. In the minutes of 1802, this Association defined valid baptism to consist in the administration of the ordinance by immersion by
*an administrator legally called to preach the Gospel and ordained as the Scriptures
direct*, and that the candidate for baptism make a profession of his faith in
Jesus Christ, and that he be baptized into the name of the Father, and of
the Son, and of the Holy Ghost, by dipping the whole body in water.''

(Signed)   "J. VARDEMAN,
         "E. WALLER,
         "JAMES FISHBACK,
         "JOHN EDWARDS,
         "JACOB CREATH.''

izing the Providence church would be considered revolutionary *"somewhere."* We have here shown that "somewhere" is not in Tennessee or the South only; but it was by all the Baptist Churches in America from 1708 to 1808—and I most earnestly pray that they may continue to be so considered until Christ returns—and let every Baptist in America and on earth say **"Amen!"**

The examples as well as the positive precepts of the New Testament are our guides in the constituting of churches; and within its lids not one example can be found of an *unbaptized* administrator, or of one who was not an official servant of a church, who presumed to baptize, save John the Baptist, who did so under especial commission of Christ in the inchoate state of His Kingdom. It was also by the especial command of the Holy Spirit that authorized Phillip, one of the seven deacons of the church at Jerusalem, to receive the experience of the eunuch and baptize him into the fellowship and membership of that church, of which Phillip was an officer. These exceptional cases are no examples for us to follow. The ordinances were delivered to the churches to be *preserved* and *observed* by them (I. Cor. xi.), and delegated trusts can not be relegated.

Certainly, intelligent Baptists can not be so "bewitched" by human opinions and sophistries, or influenced by partialities and prejudices, as to surrender these fundamental principles and thereby let in a floodtide of destructive irregularities that would, in a generation, sweep the churches of Christ from the face of the earth. God forever forbid it.

These gross irregularities are condoned and confirmed

as valid by the Providence church and its friends under the plea of *necessity*, and "necessity knows no law!" But there was no necessity in the case. There was a regular Baptist Church at Newport, only twenty miles from Providence, several of whose members lived even beyond Boston. Old Father Witter resided in Lynn, Mass., and had Mr. Williams been at heart a Baptist, he and his followers could have been baptized and received regularly into its membership, and had they wished to have constituted a church at Providence, they could have been dismissed by letter and organized one in due order. But the fact was, Roger Williams did not believe that there was a church on earth scripturally authorized to administer the ordinances, and under the influence of an imagined inspiration from Heaven, he felt authorized to originate one, but in a few weeks he saw his folly, repudiated his act, deserted his ill-gathered company, and "in four months it came to nothing," says Cotton Mather.

Now, for the sake of the Providence church and the Baptist denomination, I rejoice in being able to say that

The Records of the Providence Church are not Reliable.

I would not intimate that the misstatements and dates were intentionally made, but, in the first place, largely owing to lack of *data*, and, second, to inexcusable carelessness where the proper *data* were in hand or at hand.

I furthermore rejoice that these errors, by the diligent research of Dr. Adlam, have been made so manifest

as to leave no reasonable doubt in the mind of the
intelligent and impartial inquirer, that, I am confident,
the First Church at Providence, rejoicing only in the
truth, will take great pleasure in correcting them on
the Tablet on the wall of its church and in its Church
Records, and by publishing the fact to the world, bring
great relief to a denomination that has been so long
sorely tried in attempting to explain or defend this
most inexplicable and indefensible portion of its American history.

*Proofs of the Unreliability of the Records of the First Baptist
Church, Providence, R. I.*

Comer, A. D. 1730, the most reliable of writers, distinctly and repeatedly ascribed the priority of age to
the Newport church. Of this church he says: "This is
the First Baptist Church in Rhode Island, and the first
in America."*

Dr. Manning, A. D. 1817, who was for years the president of Brown College, and pastor of the Providence
church, says:

"During the brief period of his stay here Reverend
John Stanford gathered such facts as he could find,
and his account was inserted in the Book of Records.
It has been quoted by Benedict and other writers, as if
it had the authority of original records. **But it contains
many errors.** It was published by Dr. Rippon in his
Baptist Annual Register, in 1801–2, with a picture of the
meeting-house. The publication, for some reason, was
delayed for several years."—*Manning and Brown University,* 440.

---

* See page 19.

Dr. Caldwell, pastor for many years, in his Two Hundred and Fiftieth Historical Address, says this about the way the church records were gotten up:

"**No** *records before the coming of Manning,* **in fact, prior to 1775, have been preserved.** They may have departed with Winsor and his church, and *disappeared, we know not where.* **One hundred and fifty years of the story now told has had to be taken wherever it could be found, and not from any records preserved and authenticated by the church itself.**"

Dr. Benedict, the venerable historian of American Baptists, confesses that in making Roger Williams the founder and first pastor of the First Baptist Church at Providence, he did not go behind the church records, but accepted them as reliable; but his testimony, before he died, was: "The more I study on this subject, [*i. e.,* the date of the Providence church and the statements that Roger Williams was its first pastor and it being the First Baptist Church in Rhode Island and America,] the more I am unsettled and confused."*

The attempt to reconcile the statements of the Church Records with the *unquestioned facts of history* is quite enough to confuse and unsettle any mind — they can not be reconciled.

Dr. Adlam, in the work I am here introducing, challenges the statements of the Records with unquestioned authorities, and exposes the unpardonable ignorance and carelessness of Mr. John Stanford, who compiled them, one hundred and fifty years after the church was organized, from reports picked up here and there.

* History of Baptists, p. 443.

The one witness, Dr. Manning, pastor of the Providence church, who challenged their correctness the year they were compiled, and asserted that they contained **many errors,** is quite enough to impeach them; without adding that of Roger Williams himself! Thomas Lechford, whose testimony is of the highest authority (Adlam), being an Episcopalian and partial to neither party, visited Providence in the year 1640–41, says:

"At Providence, which is twenty miles from Newport, lives Master Williams and his company of divers opinions; most are Anabaptists;

They hold there is no true visible Church in the Bay, nor in the World, nor any true Ministry."

Mark well! this was two years after the records say Mr. Williams had founded the First Baptist Church, of Providence, and was at the time its pastor! Is it conceivable that Mr. Williams would have said this (for who but Mr. Williams informed Mr. Lechford of the state of the colony, and to whom but Mr. Williams would Mr. Lechford have applied for reliable information as to his religious opinions and those of his followers?) If Mr. Williams told the truth, the records gotten up for the church a century and fifty years after the events occurred are false. Which of the two witnesses is most likely to be correct, the one who testified from his personal knowledge of things, or one who gathers up "from here and there" vague reports a century and one-half after?

We may safely say that

Roger Williams testified that in 1641-2 there was no visible Church in Providence.

This one fact admitted by the First Baptist Church, of Providence, *i. e.*, that her records are unreliable — a fact so abundantly proved by historians, and admitted by her own most eminent pastors—and by her corrected so as to accord with the *unquestioned* date of her origin and name of her founder and first pastor, as demonstrated by Dr. Adlam in this work, and these most desirable results will follow:

First — The lips of those — and they are many — who seek a cause — if only the shadow of one — to disparage our American history, and who confidently, and with **show of reason,** charge that the records of the Providence church, and our churches in New England and largely in America and their ordinances *were originated and given to us by an excluded Pedobaptist, who virtually baptized himself,* will be forever closed—a consummation devoutly to be wished. And this will be gained, and at the expense, to the Providence church, of only three years of extremely doubtful history and the exchange of one honorable name as its founder for another not less so.

Will not the Providence church do this for the sake of exact historical truth and the peace of the denomination?

Does she prefer to walk in the dark rather than in the clear light? Does she prefer an uncertain to a certain history—a doubtful to an undoubted history?—

3

and that when her extremely doubtful history confuses and unsettles the minds of historians and brethren, and enables our enemies to use it to our disparagement, and to prejudice us in the eyes of the world; as has been done and is *now* being done all over this land, and will continue to be done until the *doubtful* gives way to the *certain.*

Second—Let the First Church, of Providence, do this, and then will no one of her future pastors be compelled to protest against the reliability of her Book of Records. "**It contains many errors**," as did Dr. Manning.

Third—Let her do this, and then on no future anniversary will her orator be compelled to say, as did Dr. Caldwell last April, 1889.

"We Celebrate, after all, an Unknown Day. There is no Record of the Exact Date of Our Beginnings." *

I will believe she will do this, until she herself convinces me to the contrary, by perpetuating the dates and statements of her Book of Records to another generation, so heavily challenged by the historians and *her own pastors* of this and former generations.

There are only two conflicting theories as to the date of the constitution and founder and pastor of the First Baptist Church, of Providence, R. I.—of course only one of them can be correct.

---

*See his Two Hundred and Fiftieth Anniversary Address, delivered April 28, 1889.

First—The first theory is, that Roger Williams constituted it in the year 1639 by immersing eleven excluded Pedobaptists, himself having been previously
immersed by one of them whom he had immersed;
which company, left without creed or covenant* or
ordinances,† perpetuated its existence until now, and
is the present First Baptist Church, of Providence,
R. I., recognizing and transmitting these indefensible
irregularities.

Second—The second theory is the one developed and
cleared of all difficulties by Dr. Adlam in the book I
am introducing to the favorable attention of the
reader, viz: That the present First Church was regularly constituted and jointly or successively served by
Charles Brown, Wickenden and Dexter in 1652 (thirteen years after Roger Williams, in the language of
historians, "had left the Baptists and had publicly
declared there was no church in the Bay that had any
authority to administer the ordinances," although he
did assert of the Baptists "that, in their faith and practices, they were nearer the apostolic churches than any
church he was acquainted with.") This latter date
harmonizes with all the well authenticated facts in
the case. The Providence church claims one or more
of the above ministers as her pastors in the lifetime
of Roger Williams!

Now, the first theory has been abundantly disproved:
that company of unscripturally, and, therefore, unbap-

---

* "Our fathers founded, and the centuries have handed down to us a
church (?) without a written creed."—DR. E. BROWN, Pastor.

† Discourse on Two Hundred and Fiftieth Anniversary, 1889.

tized individuals, was not a church—being as destitute
of an organization as of "creed or covenant." It was
soon repudiated and left by Roger Williams, and, in
the language of Cotton Mather (Presbyterian, who lived
in the town), "within four months came to nothing."*
Roger Williams, although he lived forty years after in
the city of Providence, and within twenty miles of the
First Baptist Church, at Newport, R. I., never joined
or affiliated with either.

There is no shade of evidence that Roger Williams was ever a Baptist one hour of his life.

When Dr. John Clarke, of Newport, gave his farewell charge to his brethren he warned them to beware
of and spurn both Scylla and Charybdis—Hierarchism
—the church-and-state-church on the one hand, and
anarchism*—the Roger Williamites—on the other, as
equally dangerous.*

Before presenting Dr. Adlam's history of the origin
of the first two Baptist Churches in Rhode Island
and America, that have so long contended for priority
of constitution, I deem it proper to give the reader a
brief sketch of the lives of three of the most prominent persons who lived and suffered, for the testimony
of Jesus and the Word of God, in the first century of
the history of New England and American Baptists.

---

*See Dr. Barrows' Historical Address.

Part Second

ROGER WILLIAMS.

BY THE EDITOR.

SEC. 1. *A Brief Sketch of his Life.*

He seems providentially raised up as "a herald," "a voice," to proclaim in this, then wilderness, the eternal divorcement of Church and State, and the absolute freedom of man to worship God according to his understanding of His Word, and thus to prepare the way for the coming of His Kingdom into New England and America.

Little is known of the early life of young Roger. The place of his birth is not recorded. This much is known, that Roger Williams, son of William Williams (gentleman), was baptized on the 24th of July, 1600, in the parish church of Guinness, Cornwall, England.

From this we learn that he was born and confirmed into the Church of England; his family were members of the Episcopal Church, and he, therefore, was born, or *made* a member of it in unconscious infancy. Early in life, he tells us, he was brought by God's grace to know "Christ as his personal Savior," and to realize that his Savior was also his *Lord*, and entitled, not only to the *supreme love* of his heart, but to the *supreme*

(39)

service—obedience—of his life, and that Cæsar had no right to come between his soul and his Savior.

These Puritan ideas doubtless account for the opposition of his father and his leaving home for London. His persecution commenced in his father's house, and followed him until the day of his death.

In a letter to Governor Winthrop (1632), he says: "I have been for these twenty years persecuted in and out of my father's house." He received the degree of A. B. from Pembroke College, and commenced the study of law, under the direction of Sir Edward Coke, which, not being suited to his taste or inclination, he soon relinquished, and entered upon the study of theology. He received orders and assumed charge of a parish. His decided opposition to the liturgy and hierarchy of tne Established Church (the Episcopal Church of England), as enforced by the bloody Archbishop Laud, to escape from whose tyranny he fled to the New World, carrying with him a spotless Christian character, in the hope of finding

"FREEDOM TO WORSHIP GOD."

SEC. 2. *His Settlement in New England—Troubles Ecclesiastical, and Final Exclusion from the Plymouth Colony.*

After a tempestuous passage of ten weeks he landed, with his young wife, Mary, off Nantasket, February 5, 1631.

"He was," says Cathcart, "now in his thirty-second year of his age, and in the full maturity of his mental and physical powers; a devout and zealous Christian, a ripe scholar, and an accomplished linguist—one who was accustomed to read the Scriptures in their original tongues."

He soon received a call to settle over an Episcopal Church in Boston, but declined because, as he wrote to Cotton, he "durst not officiate to an unseparated people," so thoroughly had he become imbued with that great Baptist's doctrine of religious freedom set forth in their "Confession of Faith," published in London in 1611, viz: "The magistrate is not to meddle with religion or matters of conscience, nor to compel men to do this or that form of religion, because Christ is King and Lawgiver of Church and conscience." It was from this pure fountain that Williams drank in the sentiment and principle of soul freedom, which animated and influenced his whole life.

Owing to the opposition of the magistrates Mr. Williams soon removed to Salem, and became connected with the church in that place, which was a separated— independent—body.* On the 12th of April, 1634, he was regularly ordained as its pastor.

From this period dates the controversies he had with the court and *clergy* (of the Episcopal Church, that was the *State* Church, of Massachusetts Bay at that time), which disputes, and his unyielding opposition to edicts of the magistrates, resulted in his banishment by the court from the colony. Concerning the causes of his banishment there are opposing views.

---

*Answering to the Congregational Church of this day.

The clergy and court party aver that it was solely his opposition to the civil government and gross "contempt of court," which is in England and this country to-day a very grave offense and severely punished; while his friends maintain that it was solely for his "religious opinions." That it was for both causes is, I think, clearly seen from the charges themselves that Mr. Williams admits are truly drawn.

The Charges of the Court.

Roger Williams charges this court and government:

First—That we have our land by patent from the King, but that the natives are the true owners of it, and that we ought to repent of such a receiving of it by patent.

Second—That it is not lawful to call a wicked person to swear (take an oath), or to pray, as being actions of God's worship. [This may have been aimed at the unregenerate clergy of the Church of England. to which our next charge points.]

Third—That it is not lawful to hear any of the parish assemblies of England.

Fourth—That the civil magistrate's power extends only to the body and goods and outward state of man.

Summed up by the presiding magistrate, at his final trial, by Governor Haynes. I acknowledge the particulars are rightly summed up.   ROGER WILLIAMS.

The last is the only charge that looks in the direction of "religious opinion," and could not be granted by the court without a perfect revolution of the existing government and the surrender of the Charter of the colony.

Sec. 3. *Roger Williams' Banishment from Plymouth and his Settlement in Providence, R. I.—The Character of the Government he formed—His Abortive Attempt to Organize a Baptist Church—His Invalid Baptism Originated and Died with him.*

The sentence of the court was for Roger Williams to leave the colony in six weeks, and was passed October 19th. Williams did not leave, and the officers waited on him for twelve weeks! They had no intention to drive him into the wilderness in mid-winter, but, as the season was late, to send him to England with Captain Underwood. But when the captain reached Salem with his ship, Mr. Williams, preferring to look out a new home beyond the jurisdiction of the Bay government to returning to England, he fled into the woods towards the West. Had he taken this step October 19th, when he knew he must change his location, he would have avoided the hardship he experienced in January. His journeying in search of a better home would have been a pleasant one. The Indians were all friendly to him, their chiefs his particular friends, and the wilderness quite familiar. He first rested in Seekonk, but in the June following, with five others, in a boat landed where Providence now stands. They gave it this name in gratitude to the Goodness that had so well provided for them. Others came from Massachusetts, and they entered into a "compact," "only in civil things," and thus became a "town fellowship," and subsequently—March 14, 1644—he obtained a Charter from the commissioners appointed by

Parliament for the control of colonial affairs, under which the town became a colony under the title of "Rhode Island and Providence Plantations."

Upon the religious liberty secured by these two documents is based these eulogistic words of Gevinius, the German professor:

"Thus was founded a small new society in Rhode Island on the principle of entire liberty of conscience, and the uncontrolled power of the majority in secular concerns. * * * These institutions have not only maintained themselves here but have spread over the Continent."

I submit both the "compact" and the so much lauded provision of the Charter obtained by Roger Williams, that my readers may judge how much liberty of conscience was secured to the colonists by them. A little history will help to understand the document.

In 1637, Roger Williams, having then with him four men and two youths—nearly of age—consulted a friend about his right to require of the former to whom he yielded lands [given to him by the Indians], to sign a document, which he submitted, promising active and passive obedience to the agreements of the majority. Concerning those few young men and "any who shall hereafter plant with us," (he proposed)

This Compact.

"We, whose names are hereunto written, being desirous to inhabit in this Town of Providence, do promise to subject ourselves in active or passive obedience to such orders and agreements as shall be made, from time to time, by the greater number of the *present house-holders* of this Town, and such whom they shall admit into the same fellowship and privilege."

The reader can see there is no freedom of *belief* secured to the signers by this document, certainly.

There is a copy of another compact preserved, the *fac simile* of the first save the closing four lines, for which these are substituted: "agreements as shall be made for public good of the body in an orderly way, by the major consent of the present inhabitants—masters of families—incorporated together in a Town's fellowship, and others whom they shall admit unto them — only in civil things."

There is no guarantee of freedom in this document. It constitutes the householders of Providence an absolute aristocracy, with unlimited powers to decide what is for "the public good." It is claimed that none of the first thirteen proprietors signed it, except the two youths. It was a formal submission of new-comers exacted by those who were proprietors.

" The final four words," says Professsor Clarke,* " by their clumsy connection with the document, show what is well enough demonstrated by their absence from Mr. Williams' original draft, that, instead of being a concession of the freemen, they are appended words of reservation and self-protection of the new-comers, without which they would not sign away their religious liberties."

The provisions of the first Charter procured by Roger Williams, which is claimed as securing absolute re-

*Baptist Quarterly, April, 1876, p. 20.

ligious liberty for Baptists and all other denominations in Rhode Island, are:

First—It defined the boundaries of the State, *and that so blindly as to entail a half a century of quarrels.*

Second—It included Providence, Newport, and Portsmouth, under the name of "The Providence Plantations," in one government, *in which the majority should rule.*

Third—It gave liberty to make and execute laws; provided "that *said laws and constitutions and punishments be conformable to the laws of England,* so far as the nature and constitution of the place will admit."

"But," says Professor Clarke, "the laws of England sanctioned imprisonments, hangings and burning for religious opinions, and, under this Charter, a majority could enact those in Rhode Island!" In neither of these documents did Roger Williams secure the full and free enjoyment of religious liberty for his people, or Baptists, or anyone else. For the further discussion of this question, see Part III., by Dr. Adlam.

SEC. 4. *His Abortive Attempt to Organize a Baptist Church without Baptism, "Creed or Covenant."*

The history of Mr. Williams' abortive attempt to organize a Baptist Church at Providence, already noticed in this Introduction, can be comprised in a few paragraphs.

The latent conviction that, a few months after, broke forth into open Familism, viz: that the "gates of hell" had, indeed, prevailed against the Church and Kingdom of God, and that their continuity had been lost, and,

co sequently, all authority derived from a Gospel
Church to administer the ordinances had been lost;
and therefore, if the visible church and its ordinances
were to be perpetuated on earth, they must be recom-
mended by some one under the direction of the Holy
Spirit, and believing that the Spirit moved upon him
to do this work, he, in the year 1639, influenced a
company of his followers (eleven in number) to engage
with him in this co-religious undertaking. This was
the manner of it: One of these, Ezekiel Holliman,
immersed Mr. Williams, and he (Mr. W.) returned
the kind office and immersed Mr. Holliman and *eleven*
others—all of these had been excluded from the Salem
church, not on any charge of immorality but for their
Anabaptistical opinions.*

So far as can be learned this was all Roger Williams,
or these immersed persons, did to effect the setting
up or constituting a visible church. They were left
without a shadow of organization—without creed or
covenant—without which a Scriptural Church can
not be constituted, since an organization without a
compact, based upon definite principles and laws, is
an absurdity. Rev. E. Brown, D. D., pastor of the First
Church, Providence, in the two hundred and fiftieth anniversary sermon, April 28, 1889, said: "Our fathers
founded, and the centuries have handed down to us, a
church without a written creed;"† and he could have
added covenant, constitution, or organization!

---

* This was not a case of alien immersion — baptism by a Pedobaptist
minister—since Mr. Williams and Mr. Holliman, as well as these ten, were
excluded members of the Salem—a Pedobaptist—church.—DR. CALDWELL'S
Two Hundred and Fiftieth Anniversary Address, p. 37.

† See Two Hundred and Fiftieth Anniversary Publication, p. 11.

History gives us no intimation that Mr. Williams ever stately preached, or presumed to administered the Lord's Supper to, or immersed another person into it.   He soon repudiated his work as unscriptural and null, and deserted the company—we can not call it a *church*—"and in four months," Cotton Mather, an eminent Pedobaptist minister and historian, says, "it came to nothing."   This is his statement:

"One Roger Williams, a preacher, arrived in New England about the year 1630; was first an assistant in the church in Salem, and afterwards its pastor.   This man—a difference happening between the government and him—caused a great deal of trouble and vexation. At length the magistrates passed the sentence of banishment upon him; upon which he removed with a few of his own sect and settled at a place called Providence.   There they proceeded not only unto the gathering of a thing like a church, but unto the renouncing their infant baptism.   After this he turned Seeker and Familist, and the church came to nothing."*

All authentic records fix the utter extinction of this company at four months.†   It was gathered in March, and came to nothing the following July.   Therefore,

Roger Williams' baptism originated and died with him.

He lived forty years after this, and it is a well-established fact that he never united or communed or affiliated with any Baptist Church, either in

* Mather's *Ecclesiastical History of New England*, p. 7, and Crosly, Vol. I., p. 117.

† Backus, Vol. I., p. 89, and |Scott's Letter in George Fox's Answer to Williams, p. 247.

Newport or Providence, but on the repudiation
of his "thing like a church" he became a professed
Seeker, or Familist, the cardinal principle of whose
faith was: "The true church being lost in the general
corruption, there must be a new beginning, with new
apostles, i. e., men inspired of God and authorized to
re-institute the ordinances and worship of the Lord's
House. Some of them taught that both the church
and its ordinances are to be understood in a purely
spiritual sense. They professed to be seeking more
light than they had, including a fresh revelation from
Heaven, and hence their name Seekers.* This people
were considered *Anarchists*, and were equally obnoxious
to the Baptists as were the Pedobaptists, or *Hierarchists*.

---

* "This must be the class of men — these Seekers — Mr. Clarke has in
mind when he bids men remember that 'the spirit that does not exalt
Christ, can not be the Spirit of Christ, or the Holy Spirit of promise; and
urges them to try the spirits, to bring them to the wholesome words of the
holy apostles, prophets, and the Son of God; and counsels them that it be the
Christian's care to search the Scriptures, and THEREIN to wait for the power
and glory of the Spirit of God.' He also charges the people to steer clear of
both Scylla and Charybdis, of the opinion of those on the one hand who
destroyed the purity and spirituality of the church by uniting it with the
civil power, and by introducing into it unregenerate material by infant
baptism; and of the opinion of those on the other hand who denied that
there were any visible churches. He would have them avoid both extremes;
'*not turn to the left side in a visible way of worship, indeed, but such as was neither
appointed by Christ, nor yet practised by those who first trusted in Him;* nor to
the right in no visible way of worship, or order at all, either pretending
....*that the church is now in the wilderness, or that the time of its recovery is not
yet, or else pretending that God is a Spirit, and will in spirit be worshipped, and
not in this place or that, in this way or that.*'—(*Ill News*, 4 *Massachusetts History*,
Coll., II., 19, 20.) Thus, while maintaining the spiritual constitution of the
church, he adhered to its outward form, its organic structure, and put
honor upon the Scriptures, teaching, with Chillingworth, that 'the Bible,
the Bible alone is the religion of Protestants.'"—DR. BARROWS' *Dev. Bap.
Prin. in Rhode Island*, p. 21.

4

Dr. Clarke, in his farewell address to his people charges them to steer clear of both Scylla and Charybdis of Hierarchism, Church and State religion on the one hand, and Anarchism, *i. e.*, Roger Williamites, on the other.

In reviewing his history, I confess myself at a loss to discover wherein the Baptists of New England or America are indebted to Roger Williams.

He was not the first, by a large part of a century, to assert by pen or voice the doctrine of religious liberty. He caught his inspiration from the Articles of Faith of the old Baptist Churches of England, and was educated in the doctrine by the writings of Busher and other suffering Baptists in England.

He never, by any legal document that has been discovered, embodied the doctrine of *free and full* freedom of conscience for them, or any other denomination in Rhode Island, as has been claimed. He did not insert one provision for the enjoyment of free and full religious liberty in the Charter he obtained from England —to secure which the colonists subsequently sent Mr. John Clarke.*

He was never a Baptist one hour in his life. No authentic document sustains the claim that he was ever the member of, or communed or affiliated with, any Baptist Church. The claim is utterly absurd, since in less than four months after he was immersed by Holliman he repudiated the act as *null*, and turned Seeker and Familist, denying that Christ had a visible church on earth, or that there were "any scriptural

---

* See Dr. Adlam's Historical Address, at the close of this book.

church, state, or ordinances extant." He was both by his practice and teaching a most serious obstructionist to the Baptists of Rhode Island and America.

If any one will show wherein the Baptists of America are indebted to Mr. Williams, I will most cheerfully insert it on this page, in the second edition of this book. I close this sketch in the words of Dr. Adlam:

"Among the evils that have resulted from the wrong date of the Providence church, has been the prominence given to Roger Williams. It is greatly to be regretted that it ever entered into the mind of any one to make him [a Baptist or] the founder of our denomination in Rhode Island or America. In no sense was he so. Well would it be for Baptists, and for Williams himself, could his short and fitful attempt to become a Baptist be obliterated from the minds of men. A man only four months a Baptist [and only *attempting* to become one at that], and then renouncing his baptism forever, to be lauded and magnified as the founder of the Baptist denomination in the New World! [Is simply absurd!] For all he did as a statesman to aid our brethren in the, or advocacy of the, separation of church and state, I respect him; but as a Baptist I owe him nothing."

DR. JOHN CLARKE, OF NEWPORT, R. I.,

THE BAPTIST STATESMAN.

BY PROF. J. C. C. CLARKE.

THE Colony of Massachusetts, or The Bay, having its centre at Boston, was in 1637 in a hot fermentation, being full of restless spirits, eager for and yet afraid of

all novelties in church and state. With bristling consciences and unsettled notions, they were fearful of
being in minorities, and equally afraid of organizing
their majorities. Church and state had been united
in 1631, by laws which made church members alone
eligible to citizenship, and consequently far the larger
part of the colonists were neither church members nor
citizens. Satisfied, however, with their new liberties,
the people disputed little about politics or government, but much about religion.

The crystalization of religious opinions almost immediately exhibited in Boston the three great phases
of Protestant Christianity : *First*—The host of people
which attaches itself to church organizations and ordinances, entering by infant baptism, so-called ; *Second*—
The doctrinal phase called Arminianism ; *Third*—The
doctrinal phase which bears in a restricted sense the
name of Calvinism ; but is, in fact, a strong accentuation
of the doctrines that participation in the ordinances
and church membership must follow, rather than pre-
cede, personal piety, and that in religion an acceptance
of the divine assurances by faith is the most essential
or prominent feature. In 1637, the " Independents,"
fully intrenched in the government by the laws above
mentioned, began to exhibit the germs of " The Half-
Way Covenant," and of all the later peculiar schools of
" New England Theology," and assumed an uncom-
promising attitude towards all dissenters from their
creeds or church organizations. In this year the ad-
herents of the third phase of Protestantism above mentioned found themselves nicknamed by the odious and

undeserved title of "Antinomians," and outvoted at the polls. Their favorite Governor, Sir Henry Vane, was not re-elected, their ministers were removed, and a large body of themselves were disarmed and sentenced to banishment. The party in power confessed that they were in fear of fostering Anabaptists, whom they regarded as the incarnation of rebellion and anarchy. A sweeping law of exclusion was therefore passed, forbidding strangers to even remain in the territory of The Bay more than three weeks without a governmental permit. This was the first time that there was a direct issue raised between parties in respect to "liberty of consciences," although these three words had for years been on every tongue, and men's peculiar consciences had involved them in many difficulties. When Roger Williams' conscience led him, in 1635, to use the discipline of his church to force members of the court to yield in a legislation about lands, and also led him to set churches, which were connected with the government, against other churches of the Establishment, he was not tried for his conscience or opinions, but for his acts of sedition and "contempt of court," offenses most serious in all communities, and for these he was dismissed from his church and the colony.

The history of all colonies shows that, however many may participate in such movements, only a few are leaders, putting their stamp·upon events, and leaving enduring monuments and names by force of their own characters. Boston, at this time, produced no competent leader for the despairing "Antinomians." Sir

Henry Vane returned to England. Several others, who had been high in office, in more tranquil days, now showed no genius for leadership. In this juncture, in November, 1637, John Clarke, just turned twenty-eight years of age, arrived in Boston. Immediately he counselled the "Antinomians" to unite in a movement to other territory, and his advice was adopted.

Who was this young man, so promptly accepted as a leader?

In Westhorpe, Suffolk, which was, in the sixteenth century, the seat of the Duke of Suffolk, but now is an insignificant hamlet, John Clarke's grandparents and parents lived and died, and here he is registered in the parish church as having been baptized October 8, 1609. From his early possession of considerable property, from his fine education and his evident learning in law — although specially educated in medicine, the classics and theology — and from his father's clerkly writing in the once elegant family Bible, of the Geneva version, edition of 1608, it is conjectured that his father, Thomas Clarke, was a lawyer and a Puritan. John Clarke is spoken of by his contemporaries and other early writers as a "scholar-bred," "a man bred to learning," "a learned physician." By later writers he has been spoken of as "a man of liberal education, and of bland and courtly manners," and as "one of the ablest men of the seventeenth century." He was an advanced student of Greek and Hebrew, and at his death had nearly ready for publication a "Biblical Concordance and Lexicon." The evidence is ample that he was learned in the practice of three professions,

and that he possessed those qualities of prompt and
resolute action, of courage and calmness in difficulties,
of clear-sighted and broad views, of large and philan-
thropic aims, and of winning personal manners, which
secure to their possessor respect and leadership.

In his own narrative, Dr. Clarke says:

"I was no sooner on shore, but there appeared to me
differences among them touching the covenants; and
in point of evidencing a man's good estate, some pressed
hard for the covenant of works, and for sanctification
to be the first and chief evidence; others pressed as
hard for the covenant of grace that was established
upon better promises, and for the evidence of the Spirit.
* * * * Whereupon I moved the latter * * *
for peace sake, to turn aside to the right hand or to the
left. The motion was readily accepted, and I was
requested, with some others, to seek out a place."

Dr. Clarke visited New Hampshire, but returned and
advised a more southern location of a colony. In
Boston, in the first week of March, 1638, the colony was
fully organized for emigration, its president and other
officers signed their engagements, and the permanent
state records of the body politic were begun. The first
instrument in the series is one of the most remarkable
documents in political literature, as a terse enactment
of law and liberty, recognized as necessarily united in
a government subordinated to Christ. It was signed
March 7, 1638, and is as follows:

"We, whose names are underwritten, do here solemnly, in the presence of Jehovah, incorporate ourselves into a Bodie Politick, and as He shall help, will
submit our persons, lives and estates unto our Lord

Jesus Christ, the King of kings and Lord of lords, and to all those perfect and most absolute laws of His, given us in His Holy Word of Truth, to be guided and judged thereby."

Exod. xxiv. 3.
II. Chron. xi. 3, 4.
II. Kings xi. 17.

The Scripture references, attached to this document are necessary to its interpretation. They are as follows:

"And Moses came and told the people all the words of the Lord, and all the judgments: and all the people answered with one voice, and said, All the words which the Lord hath said will we do."

"Speak unto Rehoboam the son of Solomon, king of Judah, and to all Israel in Judah and Benjamin, saying, Thus saith the Lord, Ye shall not go up, nor fight against your brethren: return every man to his house: for this thing is done of me."

"And Jehoiada made a covenant between the Lord and the king and the people, that they should be the Lord's people; between the king also and the people."

Here is, in fact, the first constitution of Rhode Island, and the first in the world, which guaranteed religious liberty. It was a constitution in that it made a corporate body, and declared the outlines of its laws, and the standard to which its laws must be adjusted. Critics have, indeed, objected that such a constitution was vague, and, in the hands of bigots, might be an instrument of religious tyranny. But the noticeable facts in regard to this constitution are, that its author has left on record elaborate demonstrations that its principles were, in his judgment, the solid and only guaranty of liberty of conscience, and the State government, organized under this constitution, immediately enacted, and ever maintained, statutes protecting religious freedom.

There is scarcely a possibility of doubt that Dr. Clarke was the writer of this constitution. William Coddington was, indeed, the first signer as the elected President and Judge, but John Clarke's name is the second. The evidence of his authorship is conspicuous in the fact that it is an epitome of those writings from his pen, which display him as the unique and almost the ideal champion of liberty of conscience in the seventeenth century. To exhibit this, or to prepare for its exhibition, we must be allowed to return a little, and then to anticipate a little, the normal course of our narrative.

English Baptists in Holland, as early as 1611, had set forth, in contrast with the vagaries of the wild Anabaptists of Munster, a declaration of principles. In this they enunciated two principles, which, taken together and properly balanced, constitute the basis of all free government. These principles are, that the people must obey magistracy; but the magistrate must not meddle with the religion of citizens.

This declaration was enunciated by a body denominated "General Baptists," holding a theory of a general redemption, and not separating themselves from communion or membership with other denominations of Christians. In September, 1633, when John Clarke was twenty-four years old, the first church in London of so-called "Particular Baptists," holding a theory of particular redemption, and withdrawing from communion with other denominations, was formed, with Mr. Spilsbury as pastor. The second was formed in 1639, and before 1646 there were many. Singularly as it may seem to some persons; but, in fact, naturally and logically, these people, so guarded in their church membership and observances, became the most pronounced defenders of religious liberty for all men. In 1643 or 1644 was printed a confession faith "of seven congregations, or churches of Christ, in London, which are commonly, but unjustly, called Anabaptists," which asserted both the duty of submission to magistrates, and the right of liberty of conscience. Dr. Clarke's connection with these Baptists is quite evident from his first day in Boston to the day of his death.

In his narative, in addition to the words above quoted, he said: "I thought it strange that they were not able so to bear each with others in their different understandings and consciences as to live peaceably together, whereupon, etc., for peace sake."

Thirteen years later Dr. Clarke, when in prison, in Boston, for religious acts done by him as a Baptist minister, while visiting in Lynn, challenged the governmental officers, and the preachers of the colony, to a debate on four theses. The next year, in London, he published a book in which he three times stated these propositions, each time with increased elaboration, until the last statement fills forty-four octavo pages. His propositions, briefly condensed, declare: *First*—Christ is King; *Second*—Baptism is dipping, and only

baptized believers may join in the order of the church;
Third—Every believer ought to use his gifts; *Fourth*—
No servant of Christ has authority over other persons
in matters of conscience. Dr. Clarke, with most cogent
logic, establishes the first proposition, and the others
flow inevitably from it. Because Christ alone is King,
all men have equal rights of liberty of conscience;
but professed servants of Christ should obey the constituted authorities. Laws in harmony with God's
laws both protect all men's equal rights of conscience,
and beneficently regulate society.

These are good evidences of the authorship of the
covenant, but there is a better one in its correspondence, with the words, which, in 1662, Dr. Clarke addressed to a king:

"A flourishing civil State may best be maintained
with full liberty in religious concernment; and true
piety, rightly grounded upon Gospel principles, will
lay in the hearts of men the strongest obligations to
truer loyalty."

The light in which we have now seen Dr. Clarke
illuminates that compact which we have called the
first constitution of Rhode Island. Seen in this light
it is a declaration of the right of all men to liberty,
subject only to the duty to respect the right of others.
We shall also see that this was the first constitution
on the soil of Rhode Island.

Early in March, 1638, Dr. Clarke, with a body of the
colonists, set out from Boston southward. Following
the natural route they found, at the head of Narragansett Bay, Roger Williams, who had come there, in the

summer of 1636, with two other men and two youths. These two men, however, had left him, and three others had joined him in 1637. Some of these were accompanied by their wives. These four men had no land by deed from the Indians, but Roger Williams claimed that the natives had promised to him personally the territory now occupied by the city of Providence. The men were all at variance in their religious and irreligious views. One, soon after, left Providence, but was during all his life a bitter enemy of Roger Williams. One was married to the undivorced wife of another man, and did not stay long at Providence. These five men, and their successors, had not a law, nor an officer, nor an organization of any kind until 1647. They were a camp in the wilderness, and had no plan to found a colony. Roger Williams afterwards wrote: "It is not true that I desired any to come with me into these parts. My soul's desire was to do the natives good, and desired not to be troubled with English company." He also wrote: "I never made any other covenant with any person, but that if I got a place, he should *plant* there with me." The name which he gave to the place, "Providence Plantations," is a perpetual memorial, that, until the summer of 1638, the settlement was not designed to be either permanent or populous. Much has been written about their having liberty of conscience, but they had it as other men camping in the woods have it when they have no organization whatever. They had "liberty of their consciences" because no one would submit to the others; but Roger Williams had not yet

declared the general right of all men to freedom of
religion, nor had he learned that religious liberty
means separation of the State from all churches, for,
in 1637, he and some of his other little company had
denied another of the body the right to a voice in
village matters, because, as they said, he restrained
liberty of conscience in that he did not want his wife
to go to Roger Williams' meetings; but he and his
friends retorted the charge of intolerance. And, in
1637, whatever organization there was at Providence
was that of an "Independent" church, and it was so
much of that character, that Williams' most intimate
friend, Governor Winthrop, did not call it a government, but a "church."

Roger Williams gave Dr. Clarke's company no invitation to stay with him. He waived them on further
south, even off the land, to the island of Aquedneck.
The suggestion suited them, and by the 24th of March
Mr. Coddington obtained, by payment of a large price,
a deed from the Indians. Roger Williams accompanied
Mr. Coddington in the negotiation, *and on the same day
obtained for himself* the first deed that he ever had from
the natives. From Mr. Williams' own letter it is shown
that Providence and Newport lands were acquired on
the same day; but the island lands were bought by a
colony, and Providence lands by an individual, the
most of them being a gift to him; that the lands of
the island colony were obtained more easily through
the known friendship of the late Governor, Sir Henry
Vane, for Mrs. Hutchinson, and others of the Anti-
nomian party who were in this colony, while he (Will-

iams) would have fared ill with the natives if he had
not deceived them. He put this, however, in this
pious phraseology: "The sachems have even conceived
that myself and Mr. Coddington were far from being
rejected by yourselves, for, if the Lord had not hid it
from their eyes, I am sure you had not been thus
troubled by myself at present."

Before the end of March, 1638, a considerable body
of colonists were established on the island, the first
town being at Portsmouth, and before the end of the
year there were there about a hundred families. All
the institutions of government were immediately organized. The president, or judge, two assistants, or
elders, a marshal, a constable, and a sergeant were installed. Provision was made for the military defense,
holding assemblies, opening highways, collecting rev-
enue, etc. Before they left Boston the judge and
secretary had signed engagements to do justice impar-
tially, according to the laws of God. Immediately on
their arrival on the island, ordinances were framed,
prescribing that laws and actions should be conformed
to "The General Rule of the Word of God," and "The
Good and Welfare of the Commonweal," and the authority of the police was limited to control of "breaches of
the laws of God that tend to civil disturbance." The
archives of the first two years have been partially destroyed, and in this destruction we have lost the record
of the first statute protecting religious liberty. In May,
1640, a revision of the laws, as customary every year,
was ratified, but is not preserved. In 1641 this declaration was made: "It is ordered that none be accounted

Delinquent for Doctrine, provided it be not directly repugnant (rebellious) to the government established," and the motto, *"Amor vincet omnia,"*—"Love will conquer all things,"—was adopted. In September, 1641, this record was made: "The law of the last court made concerning Libertie of Conscience in point of Doctrine is perpetuated." Among the first acts of the colony was the erection of a meeting-house, but the cardinal principle of religious freedom, viz: absolute separation of church and state, was maintained. Governor Winthrop records that Mr. Clarke was a preacher on the island in 1638, and elsewhere calls him "their minister." The records of the island tell a story of perpetual harmony and peace.

In contrast with the history thus recorded we notice the correspondent features of the Providence colony. Roger Williams kept the lands at Providence and Pawtuxet as his private property until October 8, 1638, six months after the island lands were partitioned. Not until that date were there thirteen landholders, and these had no organization of civil government, and no law whatsoever. Mr. Williams has left on record, in a letter to Winthrop, a document which he proposed to require any new settlers and youths on becoming of age to sign. It is a formal submission of the new settlers to the authority of Williams and his established associates. At a later date, apparently August, 1639, this document was signed by thirteen persons, all newcomers except two youths, but it was not signed as Roger Williams proposed it. Before the first signer put his name to it, he clumsily added the words, "only

in civil things," and Roger Williams and Providence
colony owe a large part of their reputation for early
advocacy of liberty of conscience to misconception of
this compact. In contrast with the harmony prevalent
on the island, the history of Providence from the first
and for many years is a story of disunion and wrang-
ling. Two other colonies went off to Pawtuxet and
Warwick, but they went in anger, and long nourished
embittered spirits. Roger Williams seems to have
been their only minister. He had been in Salem pastor of an "Independent," *i. e.*, Congregational, church.
with all the arrogance that then was often displayed in
that office. In 1639 he confessed that his mind was all
unsettled about church organization and the ordinances. The world was ringing with the protests and
appeals of Anabaptists and of the General Baptists,
but the persons of Baptist sentiments were still mostly
members of other churches. Baptist churches were
few. The first church of the Particular Baptists was
formed after Mr. Williams left England. In 1639 Roger
Williams caused himself to be immersed by Ezekiel
Holliman, and then himself immersed ten others.
There is no evidence, nor even an *old* tradition, that by
this act these persons constituted a church or formulated any protest against Pedobaptists. That was not
the custom of the day, until the Particular Baptists in-
stituted it. Even the members of the first church of
Particular Baptists in London — Mr. Spilsbury's —
remained in their membership in the Pedobaptist
Churches till 1633. In 1639 a minister of Mr. Spilsbury's church, Hanserd Knollys (Knowles), was in

New England preaching. Dr. Clarke was also probably from Mr. Spilsbury's church. But Roger Williams summoned neither of these to baptize him, and sought no affiliation with recognized Baptists. Who the persons were whom he immersed is entirely unknown. Mr. Benedict gave a list of names, but they were only the names of some landholders, copied out of a deed. Some of these were not professing Christians, and some were never Baptists! Some names of known or supposed Baptists are omitted by Mr. Benedict. The company that was immersed thus was soon after scattered. Mr. Holliman and others went to Warwick, others to Pawtuxet and Newport.

Even this baptism, and his associates in it, Mr. Williams renounced in three or four months, and repudiated all ministries and church organizations.

Dr. Clarke's leadership continued pre-eminent on the island. So rapid was the growth that the new town of Newport was established in 1639. Dr. Clarke, and most of the leading men of Portsmouth, removing thither. Mr. Coddington, as President and Judge, received the first allotment of land, and Mr. Clarke the second. Scarcely were they installed at Newport, in ——, 1639, when the Assembly voted that Mr. Clarke should write to Sir Henry Vane, to "treat about the obtaining a patent of the island from His Majesty." In 1642 the officers of the government, with Dr. Clarke, were directed again to consult about a patent for the island, and send a letter to Sir Henry Vane. If Dr. Clarke was not the leader in these plans, his associates relied on him for their execution. But these plans were frustrated by jealousy of Providence and the maneuvers of Roger Williams who hurried to England in 1643.

Sir Henry Vane, very influential in England, was an ardent friend of the Rhode Island colonists, and had been asked to procure them a patent. He probably knew little of the varied interests of the separate towns, or of Providence. In these circumstances Roger Williams, who, in 1638, had not scrupled to deceive Indians, asked for a patent from the Board of Parliamentary Commissioners, of which Sir Henry was a member, and obtained it. For this act Roger Williams has been lauded as a statesman; but, in fact, his act was a cruelty and a wrong, and the most terrible blow which the colony ever received; for the patent destroyed all existing organization, which, in Providence, was nothing, but on the island was a complete State government, which had five years of beneficent administration.

Under the flowers of the patent a chain was laid. The records of the island register the adoption of the name Rhode Island on the day before the patent was signed, and then closed forever as records of an independent State. The patent blotted our their very name, and covered them with the name of Providence Plantations, although the island had at least four times the population and wealth of Providence. The patent, evidently drawn by the law officers of Parliament, only prescribing that laws made must be conformable to those of England, defined the governmental powers of the colony only in the vaguest terms;

but it granted these powers to the three towns as towns. Hence, until the three should unite, there could be no legal government for any of them. For the credit of Roger Williams we would be glad to record some evidence, that the destructive work of the patent was unforeseen, or, at least, undesired by him, but the records are all against him. Richard Scott, the first signer of the so-called Providence compact, and whose hand probably added the four words: "Only in civil things," a man whom Roger Williams baptized, has left a record in which he represents Mr. Williams as "the forwardest in their (Providence) government to prosecute against those that could not join with him in it, as witness his presenting of it to the court at Newport."

Mr. Williams was welcomed home with an ovation at Providence, but if the indignation of outraged Christian men can ever be called lurid wrath, that term, doubtless, described the sentiments of the islanders. They rejected the patent as a hated yoke. They scorned a union with Providence, which was anarchical, and Warwick which was Gortonist, and Pawtucxet which clamored for union with Massachusetts. And to make matters worse, the people of Warwick also sent to England and secured a recognition, which separated them from the Bay and Plymouth, and included them in the patent obtained by Roger Williams. The islanders were enchained, but could do nothing. And for three years they did nothing. The records ceased, the government ceased. Nothing remained but their principles and their habits. And all the time Providence, unyielding as the rocks, insisted that if a government should be formed, it should include a legislature in which the four towns of Portsmouth, Newport, Providence and Warwick, despite their disparity of population, should have equal representations. The disorders, however, in the government of England gave no opportunity for a revocation of the patent. The necessity of organization became imperative. After three years Dr. Clarke led a majority of the islanders to accept union, but Mr. Coddington, as leader of a great body, could not, would not, join in it, and refused to fill the offices to which he was elected, and in January, 1649, he went to England to ask a repeal. To the last moment Providence insisted on equal representation as their sole demand, and instructed their representative, if this was granted, to adopt "that model that hath been lately shown unto us by our worthy friends of the island." May 19th, 1647, a government for the State was constituted, and a code of laws *prepared on the island* was ratified. The constitution and code bear ample evidences that the mind which drafted it was clerically and judicially trained. There is much reason to believe that John Clarke was its chief author. We quote its preamble:

"The form of government established in Providence Plantations is democratical; that is to say, a government held by the free and voluntary consent of all, or the greater part of the free inhabitants. * * * And now, to the end that we may give each to other (notwithstanding our different consciences touching the truth as it is in Jesus) as good and hopeful assurance as we are able touching each man's peaceable and quiet enjoyment of his lawful right and liberty, we do agree, etc."

The instrument closed with these words:

"Otherwise than thus what is herein forbidden, all men may walk as their consciences persuade them, every one in the name of *his* God. And let the saints of the Most High walk in this colony without molestation, in the name of Jehovah, *their* God, forever and ever."

Of the code of laws, Hon. S. G. Arnold says:

"We hazard little in saying that the digest of 1647, for simplicity of diction, unencumbered as it is by the superfluous verbiage that clothes our modern statutes in learned obscurity; for breadth of comprehension * * * and for vigor and originality of thought and boldness of expression, as well as for the vast significance and the brilliant triumph of the principles it embodies, *presents a model of legislation which has never been surpassed.*"

Dr. Clarke was a delegate from Newport in every assembly until he was sent to England in 1651. In 1649, 1650, and part of 1651, he also held the offices of general treasurer, and of "assistant" (magistrate), but it is worthy of note that these three years were those in which his active Christian ministry is best known.

One of the recorded evidences of this is noteworthy. Roger Williams wrote in 1649:

"At Seekonk a great many have lately concurred with Mr. John Clarke and our Providence men, about the point of a new baptism, and the manner by dipping. And Mr. John Clarke hath been there lately, and Mr. Lucar (an elder in Mr. Clarke's church), and hath dipped them. I believe their practice comes nearer the first practice of our Great Founder, Christ Jesus, than other practices of religion do, and yet I have not satisfaction, neither in the authority by which it is done, nor in the manner."

In the summer of 1651, Mr. Clarke, with two elders of his church, visited an aged member of the church, living near Lynn, Mass. Mr. Clarke conducted worship and Bible study, and Mr. Holmes baptized. They were arrested, imprisoned three weeks, and tried by the court, Governor Endicott presiding. Mr. Clarke was sentenced to a fine of twenty pounds, Mr. Holmes to thirty, Mr. Crandall to five. The alternative punishment to these Christian gentlemen, arrested in a private house of one of their own faith, was that they should be well whipped. All positively refused to pay. Mr. Holmes was whipped with thirty strokes of a triple-lashed whip. Mr. Clarke was released without any explanation, but an unauthenticated rumor was set afloat that friends paid the fine. Mr. Clarke, early after his arrest, stated to the court the four theses, of which we have before made mention, and demanded a debate with their theologians. At one time consent was given, but it was afterwards withdrawn, and although Mr. Clarke remained in jail, three days after he was at liberty, he could obtain no hearing.

Almost immediately after this event, the religious ministry of Dr. Clarke was interrupted by great political movements. The repugnance of a large body of the islanders to the union with Providence, and to the patent, continued vehement. Mr. Coddington, who had gone to England in 1649, to secure a repeal or modification of the patent, obtained in 1651 a commission for himself as Governor of the island for life. This practically abrogated the charter, which probably was Governor Coddington's chief desire, and opened the way for a reorganization. In this crisis Dr. Clarke was the sole resource of the islanders. One hundred and six citizens of Newport and Portsmouth presented to him a written request that he would go to England to remedy the existing evils. He consented and sailed in November, 1651. As soon as it was known that Dr. Clarke was going to England, the towns of Providence and Warwick commissioned Roger Williams to go also and watch over their interests. The two envoys sailed together, but their purposes were very different. Dr. Clarke represented two large towns harmonious in their mutual relations, and devoted to the orderly government which they had long enjoyed. Four years of government under the patent had dispelled some of their apprehensions, and reconciled most of them to the union. Dr. Clarke had seen the necessity of moving out the boundaries of the State as far as possible, and of maintaining the union of Providence and Warwick with the island for the common defence, as Massachusetts, Plymouth and Connecticut were using all agencies for grasping and absorbing the little State.

Roger Williams represented three towns which constantly and bitterly quarreled with each other. He also represented three parties, of which one maintained that the patent was abrogated, and wished the destruc-

tion to be permanent; one maintained that the patent
was annulled as to the island, but perpetuated on the
mainland; the other desired the restoration of the
patent. While Mr. Williams was in England, these
parties in Providence and Warwick indulged in lively
contests. Rival legislatures held sessions, and trials
for treason took place. One party's legislature wrote
to Roger Williams a proposition that he should get
himself appointed governor to secure a leadership to
Providence, but a subsequent legislature denounced
the proposition. So scandalous were the quarrels that
Sir Henry Vane wrote a remonstrance to Providence.

The difficulties in Dr. Clarke's way were immense,
but they were overcome with consummate skill and
wisdom. He comprehended all the elements involved
in most far-reaching projects, and determined to strike
for the grandest aims. His first success seems to have
been the capture of Roger Williams, who thenceforward
for several years seems to have heartily co-operated
with Dr. Clarke's friends on the island. The result
of this union was that the two envoys obtained, October
2, 1652, from the council of state a revocation of
the commission of Mr. Coddington, and a renewal of
the patent. By this means, although a large number
of citizens in all the towns held aloof or in opposition,
so that restoration of the government and laws was not
effected till two years later, yet a conservative majority
of peace-loving citizens was joined in an effort to secure
order. Dr. Clarke after this remained in England, but
Roger Williams returned home. Of his welcome at
Providence he said:

"I am like a man in a great fog. It hath been told me that I labored for a licentious and contentious people. At present I am called a traitor by one party, and, it is said, that I am as good as banished by yourselves, and that both sides wished that I might never have landed, that the fire of contention might have had no stop in burning."

He was, however, by the conservative party elected governor, in 1654 and 1655; but in 1656 the party of Mr. Coddington participated in affairs, and Mr. Williams was retired from office.

Dr. Clarke, in 1654, sent home a statement of his aims, and requested that they should be approved by the State government. His plans were formally approved without amendment, and he was appointed sole agent of the State to represent it in England. Cromwell, however, had now assumed power, and Dr. Clarke obtained from him nothing more than an autograph letter, authorizing the State to continue its established government. When Richard Cromwell succeeded his father as Protector, in 1659, Dr. Clarke's commission as Agent of the State was formally renewed. It was again renewed in 1660, when Charles II. reached the throne.

Mr. Clarke's difficulties were not smoothed by the accession of the King. Charles was furious against Presbyterians, Independents and Baptists. Bunyan lay in Bedford jail, and Sir Henry Vane was beheaded. The "Act of Uniformity" was promulgated. Hundreds of Baptists went to prison.

But Mr. Clarke neither lowered his aims, nor abated the boldness with which he pushed them. Seven addresses, written by him to the King, are said to be preserved in the British archives—and two of these have been copied and published. In the first of these he said that his constituents asked—

"To be permitted with freedom of conscience to worship the Lord, their God, as they are persuaded."

In the second address he said :

"Your petitioners have it much on their hearts to hold forth a lively experiment that a flourishing civil State may stand, yea, and best be maintained, and that among English spirits, with a full liberty in religious concernments."

At length, July 9, 1663, the royal seal was affixed to the charter of Rhode Island, and it was a document so extraordinary that no words of praise can be extravagant. From its phraseology, from its minuteness of detail, from the intimate knowledge displayed of all the interests of the colony, there can be little doubt that Dr. Clarke was allowed to draft it, and that it is essentially, or wholly, his composition.

The purposes of this chapter do not permit a detailed statement of the provisions of the charter, for it secured every desired benefit. It not only defended, but enlarged the State territory. It established the rights and privileges of the citizens of Rhode Island, in other colonies, and in England and foreign lands. It provided for military organization and carrying on war; it secured fishing privileges along the coast of New England; it provided for appeals to England; it constituted a form of government similar, in most respects,

to that which has long been in force in the colony, but
without the equal representation of towns.

Let the reader mark an unparalled fact. This charter was the constitution of Rhode Island, and although
formulated amid the convulsions of the seventeenth
century, it continued to be the constitution of the
State through all the period of growth; through the
war of independence; the formulating of State constitutions all around it, and of the National constitution—even one hundred and seventy-nine years—till
1842.

But most noticeable in this charter are its impreg-
nable defenses of liberty of conscience. Its preamble
quotes from Dr. Clarke's second address the passage
which we have given above, and somewhat more.
Then it decrees these immortal words:

"Our royal will and pleasure is, That no person
within the said colony, at any time hereafter, shall be
anywise molested, punished, disquieted, or called in
question, for any differences in opinion in matters of
religion, who do not actually disturb the civil peace of
our said colony; but that all and every person and persons may, from time to time, and at all times hereafter,
freely and fully have and enjoy his own and their
judgments and consciences, in matters of religious concernments, throughout the tract of land hereafter
mentioned, they behaving themselves peaceably and
quietly, and not using this liberty to licentiousness
and profaneness, nor to the civil injury or outward disturbance of others; any law, statute, or clause therein
contained, or to be contained, usage or custom of this
realm, to the contrary hereof, in any wise notwithstanding."

Dr. Clarke returned home in 1664. The charter was received with universal joy. The government was immediately organized. The legislature opened its records with this entry: "This present Assembly, now by God's gracious providence enjoying the helpful presence of our much honored and beloved Mr. John Clarke, doth declare," etc.

Dr. Clarke was a member of the government every year after his return until 1672, and that he was held to be the best legal adviser of the State is attested by the fact that by the first assembly he was placed at the head of a committee to revise and codify the laws of the State. In 1666 he was appointed alone to make a digest of the laws, "leaving out what may be superfluous, *and adding what may appear unto him necessary.*" For two years he was deputy governor. Often he was called on for special and important services. Three times he was appointed to go to England under certain contingencies, but did not go.

From 1664 till his death, April 20, 1676, Dr. Clarke held the place of first elder in his church. It was a time of difficulties. In their anxiety to be scriptural, many persons were becoming strenuous about laying on of hands, and kindred points, and a seventh-day Sabbath. These disagreements penetrated the First Church in Newport, and soon after Dr. Clarke's death produced divisions, but his influence helped, in the providence of God, to hold this first of Baptist Churches in America faithful to its early principles, and to preserve it as a foster mother and teacher of a great denomination.

The last act of his life was in keeping with the whole. On the day of his death he made a will by which a considerable portion of his estate was placed in the hands of trustees as a perpetual fund, of which the rents and profits are to be used "for the relief of the poor, and the bringing up of children unto learning." This fund, of which a portion was then appraised at five hundred and twenty pounds, is still performing its beneficent work, and in it John Clarke lives.

No posterity of John Clarke survived him. It is better so. Let the name belong to no unworthy child. It belongs to the ages, and to the world. Its record belongs in a sense to the best chapters of Baptist history; but far more it belongs to the history of civilization and of Christian statesmanship. Let it be said of him as a man, a Christian, and as a statesman, that in an age when all men blundered, and most men conspicuously sinned, he so lived that Mr. Backus wrote: "I have not met a single reflection cast on him by any one;" and Governor Arnold wrote: "His character and talents appear more exalted the more closely they are examined, * * * and his blameless, self-sacrificing life left him without an enemy." Mr. Bancroft says: "He left a name without a spot."

SOUL LIBERTY.

In Newport* by-the-sea,
An ancient town, and free,
   Came forth a plea,
For man's God-given right,
The world's inspiring light,
Religion's arm of might,
   Soul Liberty.

Kings heard it on their thrones,
Slaves caught it 'mid their groans,
   The Christian plea.
For freedom of the mind,
The power of none to bind,
The right of all to find,
   Soul Liberty.

In vain tyrannic law,
Issued with solemn awe,
   The state's decree;
The Higher Law uprose,
Confounding freedom's foes.
Guarding with sturdy blows,
   Soul Liberty.

From all the human race.
Up to the God of grace,
   From sea to sea,
Pour forth exultant songs,
To whom all praise belongs,
And shout, enraptured throngs,
   Soul Liberty.   HOMO.

---

* From the foregoing facts with respect to DR. JOHN CLARKE, and the fact that he and not Roger Williams was the first one in the New World to assert the full and free enjoyment of soul liberty, and secured it by Charter, I feel justified in substituting Newport for Salem.—EDITOR.

The third most important personage-actor in the planting of Baptist principles and churches in Rhode Island was

REV. OBADIAH HOLMES,

THE FIRST BAPTIST MARTYR* IN AMERICA,

AND

SECOND PASTOR OF NEWPORT CHURCH.

BY REV. C. E. BARROW, D. D.

It is a filial duty we owe to our fathers to keep fresh the memory of their personal excellencies and heroic endeavors, and to transmit to succeeding generations a record of their struggles and triumphs. For the rich inheritance we possess to-day is a legacy they left us, and was secured only through a succession of severe conflicts and signal victories. One of these heroes was Obadiah Holmes, whom Morgan Edwards calls "the protomartyr of the New World." He certainly suffered severely for his religious convictions and bore noble testimony for Christ and his truth.

We have a few hints respecting his early life. Born in Preston, Lancashire, England, in the year 1606, three years after the scepter passed from the hand of Elizabeth to that of the First James, his life opened amid the conspiracies which attended the inauguration of the Stuart dynasty. He was of a most excellent family, in good if not affluent circumstances, and he had the very best advantages for education that the

---

* Martyr primarily meant a *witness*, because in early times they generally suffered death for their testimony. The term is now generally understood to mean one who has died for Christ's truth. Mr. Holmes shed the first blood ever shed on this soil for Christ's sake.

period afforded. Of his "honored parents" he has given this beautiful description: "They were faithful in their generation, and of good report among men, and brought up their children tenderly and honorably. Three sons they brought up at the University of Oxford; but the most of their care was to inform and instruct them in the fear of the Lord; and to this end gave them much good counsel, carrying them often before the Lord in prayer." Notwithstanding these privileges, however, he was, according to his own testimony, a wayward boy. His confessions of the sins of his youth remind us of those of many another, even of the best of men, of Augustine, of Jonathan Edwards, of Andrew Fuller. His struggle was long and desperate into the light and liberty of the Gospel, for he tried many methods of salvation before that offered by Christ.

It is an interesting fact, shedding light upon his social condition and material resources—for which we are indebted to Mr. George Dudley Lawson, in *Appleton's Journal*, Vol. XV., page 726 — that Mr. Holmes "brought the first pendulum-clock to America, one of the first of the kind ever constructed." Such an article of household furniture was a luxury at that time. Its presence was indicative of culture, or wealth, or both. "It is most reasonable to look for the possession of the earliest pendulum-clocks among scientists and literary men; in fact, astronomers of the Continent seem to have monopolized them at their first construction, and that a clergyman — a learned scholar — should possess and bring to America one of the first pendulum-clocks made, is certainly within the bounds of possibility." "This ancient time-piece is one of the attractions of the Long Island Historical Society's rooms;" it is still doing good service, "ticking away to-day in Brooklyn, keeping accurate time and claiming no small meed of admiration from the curious and venerating throng who know of its existence."

It was in the vigor of his early manhood that Mr.

Holmes entered the strong tide setting towards the New World, arriving at Salem, Mass., in 1639, where he resided for six years, and was an honored member of the Congregational Church. Removing in 1645 to Seekonk (Rehoboth), he became at once connected with the Congregational Church newly formed there, and four years later — having embraced more biblical views of the nature of the church and of the ordinances—he was baptized by the Rev. John Clarke, and assisted in forming a Baptist Church in the town.

For their audacity in making this attempt to form a Baptist Church, "he and two others were presented to the general court at Plymouth, June 4, 1650, where they met with four petitions against them, one from their own town with thirty-five hands to it, one from the church in Taunton, one from all the ministers but two in Plymouth colony, and a fourth from the court at Boston, under their secretary's hand, urging Plymouth rulers to suppress them speedily." Though thus stimulated to severity, the court at Plymouth "only charged them to desist from their practice." One yielded to the entreaty; and the other two, Obadiah Holmes and Joseph Torrey, were bound over to the next October court. At this October session the grand jury found bills against them and several others, "for the continuing of a meeting upon the Lord's day from house to house, contrary to the order of this court, enacted June 12, 1650;" but there is no record of any sentence being passed upon them. A few months later they removed to Newport and became members of the First Church.

On 19th July of the following year, Mr. Holmes, with two companions, was sent by the Newport church to Lynn to visit an infirm member, William Witter, who there resided. This visit has become memorable. The three delegates — John Clarke, Obadiah Holmes, and John Crandall — were imprisoned and severely threatened. The church, learning of the rough treat-

6

ment its members were receiving at the hands of the
Massachusetts authorities, despatched to them, with
words of cheer and affection another messenger, Samuel
Hubbard, who states — and the statement has never
appeared in any published history: " I was sent by the
church to visit the brethren who were in prison in
Boston jail for witnessing the truth of baptizing believers only." We can not give all the details of this
visit of the Newport delegates, for the recital would
consume too much space. The prisoners were severally
to pay a fine, " or to be well whipped." The fine assessed
on Mr. Holmes was thirty pounds; it was the heaviest
of the three, doubtless because of his proceeding in
Seekonk, for which he had never been properly punished. And now that the Puritans of New England,
and in the light of the seventeenth and not of the
nineteenth century, possessed a far more humane, a
broader and Christlier spirit.

We find Mr. Holmes a few years later, in 1657, with
another member of the Newport church, making a visit
to the Dutch settlements at New York, possibly for
evangelizing purposes. They also touched at Graves-
end, at Jamaica, at Flushing, at Hamstead, and at Cow-
bay. During the absence of the pastor, Mr. Clarke, in
England, looking after the interests of the colony and
securing its great charter, Mr. Holmes, with Mr. Torrey,
had charge of the church; and the former, at Mr.
Clarke's death, succeeded to the pastoral office, which
he held till his own death, October 15, 1686. His remains were buried on his own land, over which his
tombstone still stands. Pious pilgrimages are occasion-
ally made to the spot by strangers visiting Rhode
Island, who cherish his memory and love the truth he
held so dear, and for the sake of which he was willing
to endure stripes.

Among the writings he left were:

1. A communication to his children, breathing a
sweet Christian spirit, in which he relates his exercises

of mind when converted, and a few details of his early life

2 A document addressed to John Spilsbury, William Kiffen, and other Baptists in London, in which he gives an account of his change of religious views, which made him a Baptist, and how greatly he had suffered in consequence from the authorities, both of Plymouth and Massachusetts; and,

3. A confession of his faith, in thirty-five separate statements, which he drew up in response to requests made by his friends and brothers, especially his brother Robert, and is of course strongly evangelical. "For this faith and profession," he says, "I stand, and have sealed the same with my blood in Boston, in New England."—EDITOR.

The cause that made Mr. Holmes make this bloody confession and the brutal circumstances connected with it, I will submit in the graphic narrative given by Dr. Banvard, in his charming book, "Priscilla."*

To visit and preach to an old member of the Newport church, Wm. Witter, who lived in the village of Lynn, near Boston, Mass., that church sent its pastor, Dr. John Clarke, Mr. Holmes and Dea. Crandall. These are the three strangers who had made the journey from Newport, and were seeking food and lodging in Boston, so graphically described by Dr. Banvard, and which I copy, that my readers may see how rigidly and unmercifully the church and state (Congregational Church) guarded its borders against Baptists:

---

* This delightful Historical Book should be in the family of every Baptist in the land. Their children would read it with intense interest, and from it learn what Baptists believed, for what they have suffered in ages past, and for what they are now reproached. Price, $1.50. Address, Southern Baptist Book House, Memphis, Tenn.

Sec. 1. *Three Strangers.*

One Saturday, in the month of July, three strangers, who had journeyed far, and were weary, hungry, and thirsty, arrived at Boston.

"Well pleased am I," said one, whose name was Clarke, "that Christian people dwell here, although in some points they differ from us."

"Yes," replied one of his companions, who wore a brown coat with long and broad skirts, and great pockets opening on the outside, "yes, this is one of the cities of Zion, and yonder I see their sanctuary," at the same time pointing to the meeting-house.

"No doubt, then, Brother Holmes,, the people will remember the words of the Saviour about a cup of cold water given to a disciple, for I feel as if a draught at this time would be exceedingly refreshing."

"I sympathize with you in that feeling, Brother Crandall," said the first speaker, "and I never saw the force of that passage of Solomon as I do now—'As cold waters to a thirsty soul, so is good news from a far country.' It seems to me I never longed for a good drink as I do at this moment."

"With me," said Holmes, "it is not so much thirst as hunger."

"Well, well, cheer up, brethren, for these Christian friends are doubtless given to hospitality, and will readily relieve our wants; and if not, we can go to the tavern, and pay for meals and a lodging, though we abound not in filthy lucre."

They now reached a house standing by itself on the

outskirts of the town. As they approached it, they noticed that a woman closed the door, as if to signify that their appproach was unwelcome.

"Perhaps," said Crandall, "she thinks we are thieves, or pirates, and that she would not be safe in our company."

"A word of explanation will remove her error."

They soon reached the house and knocked at the door; but no one opened it. They knocked again, louder than at first.

"Ye had better go long," said the shrill, cracked voice of an old woman on the inside.

"We are wayfaring strangers," said Mr. Clarke, "faint and hungry who wish merely to rest for a few moments, and obtain some refreshments."

"Ye must go then to the magistrates," replied the shrill feminine voice, "for I have no license."

"License! license! What does she mean by that?"

"We are not acquainted with your magistrates," said Clarke, speaking through the door.

"And we hope we may never be officially," added Crandall, in an undertone, which could be heard only by his companion, who smiled at the remark. "And we know not what you mean by a license," continued Clarke.

The shrill, cracked voice now came from the window. It proved to be that of the short, crooked-back, loquacious Mrs. Strangger. Putting her head out of the window she said:

"Why, la, didn't you know that the Gineral Court had passed a law that nobody should entertain stran-

gers without a partickler license from two magistrates?*
Gracious, I thought everybody knew that, for it has
made talk enough. Why, no longer ago than yester-
day, one of our godly elders refused to receive a trader,
although he had every reason to believe him a good
man—jist because he had no license, and said the laws
must be obeyed."

"Well, can thee not furnish us a little bread and
water?"

"If ye can make it appear that that is not entertaining strangers I can," replied the prudent little lady.

"Do ye not remember what is said about entertaining strangers unawares?"

"I would do it with pleasure, if I only had a license.
Our magistrates are so afraid of entertaining Anabaptists, Familists, and other heretics, unawares, that they
have passed this law for our protection."

The three strangers looked at each other with a singular but significant expression of countenance.

"Go ye, and get a permit from the magistrates, and
I will give ye the best my poor house affords."

Mrs. Strangger would gladly have admitted them for
the pleasure of having some one hear her talk, and for
the opportunity which their visit would have afforded
of picking up some new items which she could have
converted into materials for gossip; but she knew that
she was already a *suspected person*, and she feared to
increase these suspicions. Seeing, just at this moment,
one of the colonists in the distance, coming along the

---

* *Hubbard's New England*, p. 413, edition of 1815. *Benedict's Hist*., p. 371.

road towards them, she said to the strangers, in a hurried manner, and in tones indicative of fear:

"If ye would not get a poor, lone woman into
trouble, ye had better go 'long. Here are witnesses at
hand, and it might go hard with me if I let ye in my
house."

They felt the force of this appeal, and moved on.

"Strange place this," said Crandall, "where a stranger
can not have given him a crust of bread, nor a cup of
water without the permission of two magistrates."

"If the magistrates happen to be absent when
strangers arrive, I suppose they must fast and sleep
out doors until the magistrates return, and, in their
great kindness, license some one to perform the first
acts of hospitality."

"In our case," said Clarke, "it is probable that no
license would be given. If that timid old woman
assigned the true reason of this law, it was designed as
an embargo upon such as we. No one could get a
license to entertain us without telling who and what
we were; and to reveal that would be fatal to their
application. They would be forbidden to harbor us."

"Our prospects are not the most flattering; but here
comes a person who may perhaps help us."

SEC. 2. *A Singular Invitation.*

The individual referred at the close of the last chapter was no other than the brother of the mill, whom
the old lady had seen in the distance, and who had
now reached the travelers. They accosted him, told
him they were strangers, and asked him where they
could receive hospitality.

"As to that, our rulers are very jealous lest hospitality should be extended to unsuitable persons, and therefore require the license of the magistrates to authorize the virtue; but if ye will go with me I will show you where there is a house which no one will prevent you from entering, and where there is food which no one will forbid your eating. If ye understand, follow me."

There was something so original, hearty and frank in this invitation that they accepted it. They did understand, and were resolved not to compromise the stranger for his kindness. During the walk to the house the conversation assumed such a character that the parties found they were in sympathy with each other in their religious views. The walk was not long. When they reached the threshold the brother said:

"This is my house. I will neither invite ye in nor forbid ye to enter; ye may do as ye please; but as ye have commenced following me ye will probably continue."

They understood, and followed him in.

When the dinner was ready he said, at the same time preventing, with difficulty, the smiles from playing upon his countenance:

"Here is food. I will neither ask ye to taste it nor prohibit ye from eating it. Ye may do as ye please; but hungry men, with a meal before them, are never at a loss." They understood again, and were soon at work discussing, with a relish which keen hunger alone can give, the plain, but healthful diet before them. It is scarcely necessary to intimate to the reader that the object of this caution on the part of Eaton was to throw the whole responsibility of their proceeding upon the three men themselves, so that he might avoid the liability of a conviction under this arbitrary law.

During the conversation that ensued the trio of travelers understood that the colony was agitated upon the subject of baptism; the ministers and rulers were exceedingly fearful of Baptist sentiments, and were vigilant in discovering and severe in treating all of that sect.

Leaving this hospitable family, they prosecuted their journey toward Lynn, where they arrived in the latter part of the afternoon.

At a distance of two or three miles from the main village stood a small house, partly built of logs, in which resided an old man by the name of William Witter. He was a member of the Baptist Church which had been gathered at Newport. In consequence of his age he was unable to meet with his brethren at Newport, and therefore had requested his church to send some of its members to visit him. His request was complied with, and John Clarke, Obadiah Holmes and Crandall were appointed to that service. Clarke and Holmes were both Baptist ministers. Clarke was the pastor of the church. Subsequently, Holmes became his successor in that office.

Whether these representatives of the Newport church attracted attention and awakened suspicion by inquiring where Witter lived, or whether this brother had given notice that he was expecting some of his church to see him, it is difficult now to tell; but certain it is, the magistrates were alarmed, and ordered the constable to be on the alert for the apprehension of any suspicious persons. The travelers found Witter's house, and received a cordial greeting. The old man was overjoyed to see them. He little thought of the protracted and painful trials which this fraternal visit would occasion. Both parties had so much to say that conversation was continued until late in the night.

Sec. 3. *The Results of a Meeting.*

The next day being the Sabbath, and the meeting house being at so great a distance, it was proposed that they should have worship where they were, and that Mr. Clarke should preach. Father Witter would thus have an opportunity of listening to his own pastor, whom he had not been privileged to hear for a long time.

Accordingly, in that rough-built, solitary private house, social religious services were observed. After the offering of praise and prayer, Mr. Clarke announced his text. Believing, from his own experience, and from the indications of the times, that a period of unusual temptation and trial was about to befall the people of God, he had selected, as an appropriate passage from which to discourse, Revelations iii. 10:

"Because thou hast kept the word of my patience, I also will keep thee from the hour of temptation, which shall come upon all the world, to try them that dwell upon the earth."

During the delivery of his introduction, four or five strangers unexpectedly came in, and quietly took seats with the little domestic congregation. Having finished his introduction, Mr. Clarke said: "In opening this interesting passage of Holy Writ for your serious meditation, I shall in the first place show what is meant by the hour of temptation; secondly, what we are to understand by the word of His patience, with the character of those who keep it; and, thirdly, the soul-cheering encouragement which is furnished by the promise, that those who keep this word shall themselves be kept in the hour of temptation and trial."

He proceeded in his discourse with increasing earnestness, the little audience, in the meanwhile, giving the closest attention. Father Witter, sitting in an old, high-back arm-chair, in one corner of the room, was listening with tearful eyes and open mouth, as though he had not heard the true doctrine for many months. It was to him a great luxury to hear his own pastor, in his own house, treat so appropriate and comforting a subject as the one he had announced. Alas! the sweetness of the occasion was soon converted into gall. These unknown, harmless strangers, observing Sabbath worship in a remote part of the town, for the especial comfort of one of their aged brethren, had (as we have intimated) attracted the attention of the magistrates, and were destined to furnish, in their painful experience, an illustration of the truth of the text. During the progress of the discourse, two constables entered the room.

"What does this mean?" said the first. "Why hold

this unlawful assembly? Is not the meeting house good enough, nor the doctrines preached there pure enough for ye, that ye must hold a gathering of your own, to the scandal and injury of the place?"

Mr. Clarke paused in his discourse. The little audience turned their eyes with surprise and grief upon the disturber.

"Ye have no business here," said the second. "Ye must disperse, or take the consequences; and they'll not be pleasant, I tell ye."

"We do not intend, friends," said Mr. Clarke, calmly, "to break any good and wholesome laws of the land."

"No parleying," replied the first. "Come, shut up your book, and go with us; we have come to apprehend you."

"Apprehend us!" replied Clarke, with astonishment; we wish to know by whose authority. We should like to see your warrant."

"We come with authority from the magistrates; and as to our warrant, I will read it."

He then drew forth a document, and read as follows:

"By virtue hereof, you are required to go to the house of William Witter, and so to search from house to house for certain erroneous persons, being strangers, and them to apprehend, and in safe custody to keep, to-morrow morning, by eight o'clock, to bring before me."   Robert Bridges." *

During the reading of this precious paper, the hand of the constable trembled, as though he were conscious

---

* In our account of the treatment of the Baptists by the civil government of Massachusetts, we have followed the statements of Clarke, Holmes, Backus, and Benedict.

he was engaged in a bad cause. After he had finished, Mr. Clarke said :

" It is not our intention to resist the authority by which you have come to apprehend us, but yet I perceive you are not so strictly tied but if you please you may suffer us to make an end of what we have begun ; so may you be witnesses either to or against the faith and order which we hold."

" We can do no such thing."

" You may," repeated Clarke, " in spite of the warrant, or any thing therein contained."

After as much uncivil disturbance and clamor as the pursuivants of the English bishops, under Archbishop Claude, indulged in when they arrested the Puritans, and broke up their conventicles in England, the two constables apprehended the two ministers, Clarke and Holmes, with their brother Crandall, and led them away. There being no jail or other place of confinement in Lynn, the three prisoners were taken *to the alehouse.* It was a deeply affecting scene to old Father Witter to see his beloved pastor and brethren taken from his own house, prisoners, for no other offence than worshipping God according to the dictates of their own consciences. A recollection of the fact that they had visited him (and had thus been caught in the snare) by his own invitation, added to his sorrow. As the three prisoners left the house, the pastor said to the venerable man:

" The hour of temptation and trial has come, but let us keep the word of His patience, and He will sustain us in the time of trouble."

At the tavern, whilst at dinner, one of the constables said:

"Gentlemen, if you be free, I will carry you to the meeting."

To which they replied: "Friend, had we been free thereunto, we had prevented all this. Nevertheless, we are in thy hand, and if thou wilt carry us to meeting, thither will we go."

"Then I will carry you to the meeting."

To which the prisoners replied: "If thou forcest us into your assembly, then shall we be constrained to declare ourselves that we can not hold communion with them."

"That is nothing," said the constable. "I have not power to command you to speak when you come there, or to be silent."

Seeing the determination of the officers to take them to the meeting of those whose principles and practices they disapproved, Mr. Clarke repeated the course of conduct which they should feel themselves compelled to pursue.

"Since we have heard the word of salvation by Jesus Christ, we have been taught, as those that first trusted in Christ, to be obedient unto him, both by word and deed; wherefore, if we be *forced to your meeting*, we shall declare our dissent from you, both by word and gesture."

From this frank disclosure, the magistrates knew what to expect. They saw that if they took these strangers to meeting, it must be by compulsion. The prisoners would not go willingly to a meeting of those from whose principles of state-and-church government they so widely differed; they saw, moreover, that if they compelled them to go, a disturbance would be the consequence. The prisoners forewarned them that they should feel constrained, from a sense of duty, to express publicly their dissent, and the constables knew that this would at once kindle a conflagration. For a moment they hesitated; but after consultation with the tavern-keeper, they decided to take them.

The three men, whose own worship had been broken up, were now taken, without their own consent, to the meeting of the *standing order.* The congregation were at prayers when they arrived. As they stepped over the threshold, they raised their hats and civilly saluted them. A seat was then assigned them, which they occupied. After they had taken their seat, they put on their hats. Mr. Clarke opened his book, and commenced reading to himself. Mr. Bridges, who had made out the warrant for their apprehension, seeing them sitting with their heads covered, became excited, and ordered the constable to remove their hats from their heads, who at once obeyed, but not in the most amiable manner.

After the prayers, singing, and preaching were over, to which the prisoners listened without offering the least interruption, Mr. Clarke rose, and, in a respectful manner, said:

" I desire, as a stranger, to propose a few things to this congregation, hoping, in the proposal thereof, I shall commend myself to your consciences, to be guided by that wisdom that is from above, which, being pure, is also peaceable, gentle, and easy to be entreated." He

paused, expecting, as he subsequently said, that if the
Prince of Peace had been among them, he would have
received from them a peaceable answer. But the pastor, probably fearing that some difficult questions
might be asked, and a troublesome theological controversy ensue, replied:

"We will have no objections against the sermon."

"I am not about to present objections to the sermon,"
answered Mr. Clarke, "but as, by my gesture at my
coming into your assembly, I declared my dissent from
you, so, lest that should prove offensive unto some
whom I would not offend, I would now, by word of
mouth, declare the grounds, which are these: *First*—
From the consideration we are strangers, each to other,
and so strangers to each other's inward standing with
respect to God, and so can not conjoin, and act in faith,
and what is not of faith is sin; and in the second place,
I could not judge that you are gathered together and
walk according to the visible order of our Lord—"*

"Have done!" cried Mr. Bridges, with the authority
of a magistrate. "You have spoken that for which
you must answer. I command silence."

After the meeting, the trio of prisoners were taken
back to the tavern, where they were as vigilantly
watched during the night as though they had been
guilty of robbery.

The next morning they were taken by the constables
before Mr. Bridges, who made out their mittimus, and
sent them to the prison at Boston, there to remain
until the next county court.

* There was little of pulpit affiliation here, or ministerial or Christian
courtesy!

This mittimus charged them with "being at a private meeting in Lynn on the Lord's day, exercising among themselves—offensively disturbing the peace of the congregation at the time of their coming into the public meeting in the time of prayer in the afternoon, with saying and manifesting that the church in Lynn was not constituted according to the order of our Lord, with *suspicion* of having their hands in rebaptizing one or more among them, and with refusing to put in sufficient security to appear at the county court."

In addition to these charges, it was alleged against Mr. Clarke, that he met again the next day after his contempt, as they called it, of their public worship, at the house of Witter, and in contempt of authority, being then in the custody of the law, did there administer the sacrament of the Lord's supper to one excommunicated person, to another under admonition, and to a third that was an inhabitant of Lynn, and not in fellowship with any church; and yet, upon answer in open court, did affirm that he never rebaptized any.

They were all three found guilty. Mr. Clarke, the pastor, was fined twenty pounds, equivalent to about eighty dollars, or to be well whipped. He desired to know by what law of God or man he was condemned. The governor, who did not deem it beneath his dignity to be present on this important occasion, stepped up, and, with much earnestness, said to Mr. Clarke: "You have denied infants baptism. *You deserve death.* I will not have such trash brought into my jurisdiction. You go up and down, and secretly insinuate

7

unto those that are weak; but you can not maintain it before our ministers. *You may try and dispute with them.*" To this violent harangue of the chief magistrate of the colony Mr. Clarke would have replied at length, but the governor commanded the jailer to take the prisoners away. They were accordingly all three remanded to prison.

Sec. 4. *A Challenge.*

During his confinement that night, Mr. Clarke thought much of the insinuations which had been thrown out against him by the governor the day before, and especially of the challenge which had been given him to discuss the question of baptism. It seemed to him as if the great Head of the church had placed him in that position that there he might be a defender of the truth. He looked upon it as a most favorable opportunity to remove the various aspersions which had been unjustly cast upon the Baptists, and show that in doctrine and practice they were true Christian men. By speaking in behalf of his brethren, it appeared to him that he might possibly be the instrument of removing the unjust disabilities to which they were subject, but especially that he might, by presenting the arguments for their peculiar belief, and their objections to infant sprinkling, be the means of opening the eyes of others, and convincing them of the truth. Yet when he thought of his own inability to do full justice to the subject, and of the disadvantages under which he would labor in having the ministry of the standing order and the government arrayed against him, his heart sunk within him. "But will not the Saviour be with me? Have I not faith to believe that, according to His own promise, it will be given me in that same hour what I ought to speak?" The taunting permit of the governor, "You may try and dispute with the ministers," was constantly ringing in his ears. He offered earnest prayer for direction and assistance, and finally resolved that, by the grace of God, he would accept the governor's challenge. He did not, as a Christian minister, dare to refuse.

Accordingly, the next morning he addressed a document to the court which had condemned him, accepting the governor's proffer of a public discussion of the points at issue between the Congregationalists and the Baptists, and asking the appointment of a time and place for the occasion. This threw the court into a peculiar position. A prisoner, who had been condemned and sentenced mainly for his religious views and practices, but to whom the governor had thrown down the gauntlet for a discussion, had accepted the challenge. For the court to refuse its sanction would be a tacit rebuke of the governor, and a silent admission of the weakness, or their fear of the weakness, of their cause.

After much ado, therefore, Mr. Clarke was informed by one of the magistrates that the disputation was granted, and the time fixed for it was the next week. When this became known to the ministers of the colony, it created great excitement among them. They disapproved the arrangement. They had no wish to enter upon the discussion; they desired to have it abandoned. They therefore saw the government, and earnestly besought them to avoid it; but it seemed too late. They had gone too far to make an honorable retreat. But finding the ministers so averse to a disputation, the magistrates had Mr. Clarke brought into their chamber, and there endeavored to change the issues between him and them. They inquired whether he would dispute upon the things contained in his sentence, and maintain his practice; "for," said they, "the court sentenced you not for your judgment and conscience, but for matter of fact and practice." But Mr. Clarke was not to be misled by any partial or erroneous statements of the matter; neither was he willing that such statements should go unrebutted. He therefore manfully replied to these magistrates:

"You say the court condemned me for matter of fact and practice; be it so. I say the matter of fact and practice was but the manifestation of my judgment and conscience, and I maintain that that man is void of judgment and conscience who hath not a fact and practice which correspond therewith." He then continued: "If the faith and order which I profess is according to the Word of God, then the faith and order which you profess must fall to the ground; but if your views of truth and duty are scriptural, mine must be erroneous. We can not both be right." To these statements the magistrates apparently assented.

Although Mr. Clarke had been informed that the disputation had been granted, and the time appointed, yet it was all *informal* and unofficial. He desired to obtain an official permit, or order, for the discussion, under the secretary's hand. He would then, he felt, be protected; otherwise, the debate might be referred to as evidence of his being a disturber of the State, and a troubler of Israel. He therefore availed himself of the opportunity which was furnished by this private interview with the magistrates, to say to them that if they would be pleased to grant the motion for the public disputation *under the secretary's hand*, he would draw up three or four propositions, embracing the points which he presented in his defence before the court, and would defend them against any one whom they might choose to dispute with him, until, by arguments derived from the Word of God, he should be removed from them.

"In case your speaker convinces me that I am in error," said Mr. Clarke, following up the subject, so as to reach some definite practical point, "then the disputation is at an end; but if not, then I desire the like liberty, by the Word of God, to oppose the faith and order which he and you profess, thereby to try whether I may not become an instrument in the hand of God to remove you from the same."

To this the magistrates replied: "The motion certainly is fair, and your terms like unto a practiced disputant; but, as the matter in dispute is exceeding weighty, and as we desire that in the controversy all may be said that can be, we propose, therefore, to postpone it to a later day."

Poor Clarke was therefore taken back to prison, to wait for the arrival of this "later day."

SEC. 5.   *Fundamental Propositions.*

During this period of delay for the accommodation of the Congregational clergy, Clarke, though kept a prisoner, was not idle. He applied himself to the proposed service of drawing up the propositions which he had pledged himself to the magistrates to defend. These propositions, or theses, were four in number.

THE FIRST

asserted that Jesus Christ, the anointed One, was the great Head of His church ; that as the anointed Priest, He alone had made atonement for sin — as the anointed Prophet, His teachings were authoritative ; that as the anointed King, He had gone to His Father for His glorious kingdom, and would ere long return again ; and that it is His PREROGATIVE ALONE *to make laws and ordinances for the observance of the church, which* NO ONE HAS ANY RIGHT TO ALTER.

THE SECOND

asserted that baptism, or immersion in water, is one of the commandments of the Lord Jesus Christ, and that the only proper person to receive this ordinance is the penitent believer in Christ.

THE THIRD

maintained that it was both the privilege and duty of every such believer to improve the talents which God hath given him, and in the congregation may either ask for information to himself, or may speak " for the edification, exhortation, and comfort of the whole ; and out of the congregation, at all

*times, upon all occasions, and in all places, he ought to walk
as a child of light, justifying wisdom with his ways, and
reproving folly with the unfruitful works thereof, provided
all this be shown out of a good conversation, as James speaks,
with meekness of wisdom."*

THE FOURTH

was in the following language:

"*I testify that no such believer or servant of Christ Jesus
hath liberty, much less authority, from his Lord, to smite his
fellow-servant, nor yet with outward force, or arm of flesh, to
constrain or restrain his conscience—no, nor yet his outward
man for conscience sake, or worship of his God, where injury
is not offered to the person, name, or estate of others, every
man being such as shall appear before the judgment seat of
Christ, and must give account of himself to God, and therefore ought to be fully persuaded in his own mind for what
he undertakes, because he that doubteth is damned if he eat,
and so also if he act, because he doth not eat or act in faith;
and what is not of faith is sin."*

These points Clarke resolved, in the strength of
Christ, to defend with all his ability.

The next day, as the first rays of the morning sun
were gilding the hill tops, and drinking the early dew,
one of the magistrates of Boston visited the prison.
Having aroused the jailer, he asked to be admitted to
an interview with Clarke. After being introduced to
the cell of the imprisoned Baptist, he inquired if the
conclusions which he intended to advocate were drawn
up. Mr. Clarke informed him that they were. He
asked for a copy of them. Mr. Clarke demurred. No

official sanction had yet been given to the anticipated controversy, and he was unwilling that his conclusions or propositions should be known until that point had been gained. The magistrate urged him with much importunity to part with a copy of them; but he refused until the promise was given him that the motion for the disputation *should be granted officially*, under the secretary's hand. He then complied with the urgent request of his early visitor. Whilst Mr. Clarke was expecting this official permit, and was preparing for the public discussion by the diligent study of the Bible, he was greatly surprised by being informed by the jailer that the order for his release from prison had come.

Some friends had, without his consent, and contrary to his judgment, paid his fine, and secured his discharge.

As it was generally known that a public disputation was at hand, in which the points of difference between the Congregationalists and Baptists were to be discussed, as rumor said, between Mr. Clarke on one side and Mr. Cotton on the other, great expectations had been raised as to the result. Clarke, being fully convinced that if this disputation did not come off, the responsibility of the failure would be attributed to him, and inferences be drawn unfavorable to his side, as if his brethren feared the results of the discussion, and therefore paid his fine, so that he might return to Newport, and thus not be on hand for the controversy, immediately prepared an address, in which he stated that if the honored magistrates or general court of the colony would grant his former request, under the secretary's hand, for the disputation, he would cheerfully embrace it, and would come from Newport to defend the opinions he had professed. Having in this manner evinced a willingness to meet his opponents at any time they might appoint, he threw the whole responsibility of the failure, in case there should be any, upon them. By so doing, he maintained his own manliness, and gave public evidence that neither he nor his friends had any fear of exposing their principles to the closest scrutiny.*

SEC. 6. *A Great Change—A Dilemma.*

During the progress of the exercises at Cambridge on the next day, a man was wandering along the shore on the Boston side of Charles River. He was anxious to cross, but unfortunately all the spare boats that belonged to the citizens of the little town were on the Cambridge side, having been used in conveying visitors to the college. Finally an Indian, who had been out fishing in the harbor all the morning, came, on his way home, sufficiently near the shore to be hailed. The man called to him, and by signs engaged him to paddle him across the stream in his birchen canoe. Having arrived on the other side, the passenger hastened to the college, and placed in the hand of one of the magistrates a letter; it was the offer of Clarke to come to Newport, and engage in the much-

* How like what Baptists have to meet in our day challenges by their religious opponents, who find it so their interests to decline, but invariably lay the blame of it on the Baptists!—EDITOR

talked-of discussion. It was not a welcome document.
The advocates of infant sprinkling did not wish to
meet Mr. Clarke in an oral argument. They knew
that that rite was safe so long as it was protected by
the sword of State; but they could not foresee what
results would grow out of a public disputation. Still,
as the governor had been the first to propose such a
disputation, and the magistrates had assured Mr.
Clarke it would be granted, they were in a dilemma
what course to pursue so as to avoid the discussion
without a compromise of character, or without a tacit
implication of the weakness of their own side. The
ministers and magistrates conversed upon the subject
after the reception of Clarke's letter at Cambridge with
great interest. The object of the consultation was to
devise some way to extricate themselves from their
position without yielding any advantage to the Baptists.

Finally the minister of Boston, Mr. Cotton, who was
more strongly opposed to the public controversy than
some of the others, drew up a reply to send back, in
which he stated that Mr. Clarke had misunderstood the
governor, who had not enjoined or counselled a public
disputation, but had simply expressed the opinion
that if Mr. Clarke would confer with the ministers
upon the subject of infant baptism, they would satisfy
him of the propriety of the practice, and he would not
be able to maintain his own views before them; that
this was intended for Clarke's information privately,
but by no means as a challege to dispute publicly upon
the subject. "Nevertheless," continued this ingenious

divine, "if you are forward to dispute, and that you will move it yourself to the court or magistrates about Boston, we shall take order to appoint one who will be ready to answer your motion, you keeping close to the questions to be propounded by yourself, and a moderator shall be appointed also to attend upon that service; and, whereas, you desire you might be free in your dispute, keeping close to the points to be disputed on, without incurring damage by the civil justice, observing what hath before been written, it is granted. The day may be agreed if you yield the premises."

This was signed by the governor, Mr. Endicott; the deputy governor, Mr. Dudley, and three others. Mr. Clarke regarded it as a singular document, and understood its practical bearing. He viewed it as an attempt to change the entire ground of procedure, and shelter the governor from the charge of having proposed the discussion. In the expression of a willingness to grant the discussion, provided Clarke would move it himself to the court or magistrates about Boston, he discovered an attempt to throw the whole responsibility of the disputation upon himself, and to make it appear to result from his "forwardness to dispute."

Two other remarkable features connected with this affair, which increased the cautiousness of Clarke's movements, were: First, that while this letter of Cotton's was signed by five colonial dignitaries, it was not an order of court—it was not an official document. It was signed by them in their private capacity, and had not the signature of the secretary. Mr. Clarke, therefore, did not regard it as a reliable State paper.

The other remarkable circumstance was, that this attempt to throw the whole responsibility of originating the discussion of infant baptism upon Clarke was made, when they knew that there was a law of the colony which ordered that " if any person or persons shall openly condemn or oppose the baptizing of infants, and shall appear to the court wilfully and obstinately to continue therein, after due time and means of conviction, every such person or persons shall be sentenced to banishment."

Clarke knew that their unofficial document would afford him no legal protection, and that in case the disputation went on in the manner they proposed, it would be an easy thing for some one to enter a complaint against him, and secure his conviction. He therefore wrote the following frank and manly epistle, and forwarded it to them:

To the honored Governor of the Massachusetts and the rest of that Honorable Society, these present.

WORTHY SENATORS:

" I received a writing, subscribed with five of your hands, by way of answer to a twice-repeated motion of mine before you, which was grounded, as I conceive, sufficiently upon the governor's words in open court, which writing of yours doth no way answer my expectation, nor yet that motion which I made; and, whereas (waiving that grounded motion), you are pleased to intimate that *if I were* forward to *dispute*, and would move it myself to the court or magistrates about Boston, you would appoint one to answer my

motion, etc.,—be pleased to understand that, although
I am not backward to maintain the faith and order of
my Lord, the King of saints, for which I have been
sentenced, yet am I not in such a way so forward to
dispute, or move therein, lest inconvenience should
thereby arise. I shall rather once more repeat my
former motion, which if it shall please the honored
general court to accept, and under their secretary's
hand shall grant a free dispute, without molestation
or interruption, I shall be well satisfied therewith;
that what is past I shall forget, and upon your motion
shall attend it; thus desiring the Father of mercies not
to lay that evil to your charge, I remain your well-
wisher,   "JOHN CLARKE."

To this fair and honorable proposal of Mr. Clarke,
the governor and magistrates to whom it was addressed
thought it the wisest policy to return no answer. The
matter was accordingly dropped by their silent retreat.
Thus ended the unfortunate challenge of the governor
and the persecution of the pastor of the Newport Baptist Church.

SEC. 7. *Inward Life.*

It is time that we inquire into the fate of Mr. Clarke's
companions. Mr. Crandall, who was sentenced to a
fine of five pounds for being one of the company, was
released upon promising that he would appear at their
next court. But they did not let him know when the
next court would sit until it was over; and as he was
not present according to his promise, they obliged the
keeper to pay his fine.

With poor Holmes it fared far worse than with either of the others. He had been sentenced to pay a fine of thirty pounds, by the first day of the next court, or else to be *well whipped*, and to remain in prison until he provided sureties for the fine. Sureties he would not furnish, because he was determined not to pay the fine. Consequently, he was kept in prison. At the time of his trial before the court of assistants, when the above cruel sentence was passed against him, he replied:

"I bless God I am counted worthy to suffer for the name of Jesus;" at which one of the ministers (Mr. John Wilson) so far forgot the sacredness of his office, and the sanctity of the place, as to raise his hand, and strike him in open court, at the same time saying: "The curse of God go with thee." *

During the continuance of the imprisonment of Clarke and Crandall, Holmes enjoyed their company. This was a source of unspeakable comfort. The conversation, the sympathy, and the prayers of his fellow-prisoners assisted to banish the despondency and gloom which would otherwise have oppressed him. But after their deliverance, and when he was left alone, he was greatly distressed in spirit. In his own account of it, he said: "After I was deprived of my two loving friends, the adversary stepped in, took hold of my spirit, and troubled me for the space of an hour, and then the Lord came in and sweetly relieved me, causing me to look to Himself; so was I staid and refreshed in the thoughts of my God."

---

* Holmes' Letter, in Backus and Benedict.

As friends had paid the fines of the other two prisoners, and had secured their release, it seemed a hard case
that he should be left to feel the scourge. Brethren who
sympathized with him, resolved that he should not.
Strongfaith Bates, Stephen, the brother of the mill, and
a few others, raised, by a contribution among themselves, enough to pay his fine. But Holmes would not
permit it. In reply to their kind offer, he said:

"I dare not accept of deliverance in such a way.
And though I greatly thank you for your kindness,
and would acknowledge, with gratitude, even a cup of
cold water, yet I desire not that you should yield to
the unrighteous demands of my persecutors. Having
committed no crime, I will not permit my friends to
pay a single farthing for me."

The first day of court was drawing near, when, if the
fine was not paid, the substitute would be exacted in
stripes, and groans, and blood.

Though Holmes was strongly convinced of the truth
of Baptist sentiments, for which he was imprisoned,
and was conscientiously opposed to the payment of the
fine, or to the doing of anything else voluntarily, as a
penal requisition, yet he was nowise ambitious of the
honors of the whipping post. He shrunk with dread
from the sufferings of the scourge. He knew that,
when the court of assistants sentenced one to be " well
whipped," it meant something, and would be executed
to the very letter. Yet the night preceding the infliction of the sentence he passed in sweet, refreshing sleep.
In the morning, notwithstanding they knew that they
would provoke the wrath of "the powers that be,"

Strongfaith and Stephen, with several other friends, called at the prison to comfort and encourage the *criminal!* After appropriate religious conversation and prayer that God would give strength to suffer, and especially that he would open the eyes of the persecutors to see and love the truth, Strongfaith took from a basket, in which he had stowed a variety of comforts for the poor prisoner, a bottle of old Madeira wine. Pouring out some in a glass, he offered it to Holmes.

"No, brother. I thank you for your kindness, but I shall take no strong drink until my punishment is over, lest, if I have more strength, courage, and boldness than ordinarily could be expected, the world should say that I was drunk, or that I was carried through by the strength and comfort of what I had taken. No; let me so suffer that, if I am sustained, God shall have the glory."

Still, the prisoner was by no means certain that he would not shrink, faint, or show signs of physical cowardice, though he thus spake. Instead, however, of strengthening himself with wine and other luxuries, which had been brought, he left his friends to be entertained with each other, whilst he withdrew into another room, to hold communion with his Lord. So soon as he had retired by himself, he was overwhelmed with the deepest gloom. He was tempted to question his own sincerity and the purity of his motives. A something within, which he attributed to satanic agency, said : "Remember thyself, thy birth, thy breeding, thy friends, thy wife, children, name, credit. Thou art dishonoring all these by thy public scourging. Is this necessary when others are ready to save thee from suffering, and thy friends from disgrace?" His heart sunk within him. The idea of dishonoring any who were dear to him was more painful than the anticipated punishment; but presently the thought occurred to him, or, as he afterwards expressed it : "There came in sweetly, from the Lord, as sudden an answer: ' 'Tis for my Lord; I must not deny Him before the sons of men, (for that were to set men above Him,) but rather lose all; yea, wife, children, and mine own life also.'" This, however, did not afford him permanent peace; for soon a series of questions rushed into his mind, creating confusion of thought, and reviving his disquietude of feeling. " Is it for the Lord that you are about to suffer? Have you His glory alone in view? Is it not rather for your own, or some others' sake? Is it not obstinacy or pride ? Is it not resentment or bigotry? Is not selfishness at the bottom ?"

These unwelcome, and, as they seemed to him, involuntary queries increased his distress; but, after a jealous and careful scrutiny of his motives, he was convinced, as he said, that : " It was not for any man's case or sake in this world, that so I had professed and practised, but for my Lord's case and sake, and for Him alone; whereupon my spirit was much refresht."

He was also greatly comforted by the following passages of Scripture, which were sweetly suggested to his mind :

"Who shall lay anything to the charge of God's elect" ?

"Although I walk through the valley of the shadow of death, I will fear no evil, for thou art with me; thy rod and thy staff they comfort me."

"And he that continueth to the end shall be saved."

8

But anon, the thoughts of the terrible scourge occurred to him, and he feared that the severity of the dreadful punishment would be too much for his sensitive flesh. The disgrace of the punishment he regarded not. That belonged to others, and not to himself. Like his Lord and Master, he despised the shame. But the anticipated pain of the heavy blows made him shrink. He knew his weakness and sensitiveness, and feared that he would be overcome. Again he betook himself to the throne of grace. He prayed earnestly that the Lord would be pleased to give him a spirit of courage and boldness, a tongue to speak for Him, and strength of body to suffer for His sake, and not to shrink from the strokes, nor shed tears, lest the adversaries of the truth should blaspheme and be hardened, and the weak and feeble-hearted be discouraged. His prayer was followed with fresh consolation and strength. It produced a state of trustful submission to God, causing him to yield himself, soul and body, into the hands of his Saviour, and leave the whole disposing of the affair with Him.

SEC. 8.   *An Affecting Scene.*

When the time arrived for the condemned Baptist preacher to be led forth to punishment, and the voice of the jailer was heard in the prison, Holmes listened to it with a degree of cheerfulness. Taking his Testament in his hand he went forth with him to the place of execution. As he approached the whipping post, around which were gathered a crowd of spectators, he calmly saluted them. Two of the magistrates were present to see that the whipper did his duty—Mr. Increase Nowel, who had signed the sentence, and Mr. Flint. After waiting some minutes in expectation of the governor's coming, Nowel commanded the executioner to do his office.

"Permit me," said Holmes, as the executioner seized him, "to say a few words."

"Now is no time to speak," replied Nowel. But Holmes was unwilling to suffer in silence. He desired to declare to the multitude the grounds of his belief, and the reasons of his punishment. He, therefore, lifted up his voice and said:

"Men, brothers, fathers and countrymen, I beseech you give me leave to speak a few words, and the rather because here are many spectators to see me punished, and I am to seal with my blood, if God give strength, that which I hold and practice in reference to the Word of God and the testimony of Jesus. That which I have to say, in brief, is this: Although I am no disputant, yet, seeing I am to seal with my blood what I hold, I am ready to defend by the word, and to dispute that point with any that shall come forth to withstand it."

Magistrate Nowel told him, "Now is no time to dispute."

"Then," continued Holmes, "I desire to give an account of the faith and order I hold." This he uttered three times. But Magistrate Flint cried out to the executioner, "Fellow, do thine office, for this fellow would but make a long speech to delude the people."

In compliance with this authoritative mandate, the executioner roughly seized Holmes, and began to strip off his clothes. The sentence was to be inflicted upon the prisoner, not upon his garments. But Holmes was determined to speak if possible. Whilst, therefore, the whipper was removing his clothes, and preparing him for the lash, he said to the people:

" That which I am to suffer for is the Word of God and the testimony of Jesus Christ."

" No," replied Magistrate Nowel, "it is for your error, and going about to seduce the people."

" Not for my error," said Holmes, "for in all the time of my imprisonment, wherein I was left alone (my brethren being gone). which of all your ministers in all that time came to convince me of an error? and when, upon the governor's words, a motion was made for a public dispute, and upon fair terms so often renewed and desired by hundreds, what was the reason it was not granted?"

This was a close and significant question. As all the multitude knew that a public disputation had been anticipated, but had not yet taken place, the inquiry of Holmes seemed to demand an answer. Nowel therefore replied:

" It was the fault of him who went away and would not dispute," referring to Clarke; but this, as we have already shown, was not the case.

Flint became impatient at this colloquy, and repeated his order to the executioner:

" Fellow, do thine office."

Holmes, however, would not remain silent. Whilst being disrobed, he said :

"I would not give my body into your hands to be thus bruised on any other account whatever; yet now I would not give the hundredth part of a wampum-peague* to free it out of your hands."

"Unbutton here," said the executioner, as he gave his jacket a jerk.

"No," said Holmes; "I make as much conscience of unbuttoning one button as I do of paying the sentence of thirty pounds. I will do nothing towards executing such an unjust law."

Faithful to his word, he would not voluntarily assist the executioner in the least in removing his garments from his back.

He was as helpless as if he were asleep, and the executioner had to handle him as though he were a statue. Still he continued addressing the people.

"The Lord," said he, "having manifested His love towards me, in giving me repentance towards God and faith in Christ, and so to be baptized in water by a messenger of Jesus, in the name of the Father, Son and Holy Spirit, wherein I have fellowship with Him in His death, burial and resurrection, I am now come to be baptized in afflictions by your hands, that so I may have further fellowship with my Lord, and am not ashamed of His sufferings, for by His stripes am I healed."

The executioner having removed so much of his garments as would hinder the effect of the scourge, and

* The sixth part of a penny.

having fastened him to the post, seized a three-corded whip, raised his hands, and laid on the blows in an unmerciful manner.* Stroke followed stroke as rapidly as was consistent with effective execution, each blow leaving its crimson furrow, or its long blue wale in the sufferer's quivering flesh. The only pause which occurred during the infliction of this barbarous punishment was when the executioner ceased a moment in order to spit in his hands, so as to take a firmer hold of the handle of the whip, and render the strokes more severe. This he did three times. During the infliction of his painful scourging, Holmes said to the people:

"Though my flesh and my spirit fail, yet God will not fail." The poor sufferer did not fail. He found that his strength was equal to his day. Though the lash was doing its bloody work upon his sensitive flesh, yet his spirit was sustained by heavenly consolations. In his own account of his experience during this dreadful ordeal, Holmes subsequently said:

"It pleased the Lord to come in and fill my heart and tongue as a vessel full, and with an audible voice I brake forth, praying the Lord not to lay this sin to their charge, and telling the people that now I found He did not fail me, and therefore now I should trust Him forever who failed me not; for in truth, as the strokes fell upon me, I had such a spiritual manifestation of God's presence as I never had before, and the outward pain was so removed from me that I could well

---

* This was the sweet Christian Communion Pedobaptists have ever offered to Baptists when they had the power to inflict it.—SEE LETTER.

bear it, yea, and in a manner felt it not, although it was grievious, as the spectators said; the man striking with all his strength, spitting in his hand three times, with a three-corded whip, giving me therewith thirty strokes."

After the requisite number of blows had been given, equaling the number of pounds that he was fined, (from which we learn that, according to the Puritan standard of penal measure, one blow of a three-corded whip, well laid on, was an equivalent to one pound sterling), the cords which fastened him to the whipping post were untied, and he was set at liberty. With joyfulness in his heart and cheerfulness in his countenance, he turned to the Magistrates Flint and Nowel, and said :

" You have struck me as with roses." But not wishing them to imagine that he regarded the punishment as literally light, nor that he was sustained by his own strength, he added:

"Although the Lord hath made it easy to me, yet I pray God it may not be laid to your charge."

The crowd now gathered around him, some from mere curiosity, others inwardly rejoicing that the heretic had been scourged, whilst a third class were filled with mingled emotions of sympathy with his sorrows, and indignation at his wrongs.

SEC. 9. *Effects of Persecution.*

Amongst those whose feelings of sympathy and indignation were aroused at the barbarous treatment of Holmes, were two individuals who were so rejoiced that the sufferer had been sustained under his cruelties, and that he left the ignominous post with so much composure, and even with pleasantness of countenance, that they shook hands with him; and one of them, whose name was John Spur, a freeman of the colony, said to him, "Blessed be God for thee, my brother," and walked along with him to the prison. The other, who simply shook hands with him, was another free-man, Mr. John Hazel. Many others testified their friendship for him, and glorified God on his account. To some, however, who were present, these expressions of sympathy were extremely displeasing. They looked upon it as a connivance at the crime, and a contempt of the government. As informers, they immediately made complaint of what they had witnessed, and a number of warrants were issued for the apprehension of these sympathizing offenders.

When Holmes reached the prison, his body was found to be in a terrible condition—his body, not simply his back, for the lashes of the whip were so long that they lapped over his back, and left their gory marks upon his side.

Eaton who had been a spectator of all the proceedings, ran home immediately after the whipping, obtained some rags and oil, and hastened to the prison where, like the good Samaritan, he dressed the wounded man's sores. When it was known that Holmes had received such kindness, the inquiry became general, who was the surgeon. And the report was soon circulated that he was to be arrested.

So severe was the chastisement of the prisoner that

for many days he could not endure the pain occasioned by the wounded parts of his body touching the bed. *All the rest that he experienced was such as he obtained by supporting himself upon his knees and elbows!*

The day after the whipping, whilst Spur and Hazel were attending to their business, they were surprised by a constable calling upon them and telling them they were prisoners. As his authority, he showed them the following document:

"*To the keeper or his deputy:*

By virtue hereof, you are to take into your custody and safe keeping the body of John Spur, for a heinous offence by him committed; hereof fail not. Dated the 5th of the 7th month, 1651. Take also into your safe keeping John Hazel.

By the court,   INCREASE NOWEL."

They were accordingly both taken to prison, the *heinous offence* consisting of the act of shaking hands and speaking with Holmes after his punishment, and, consequently, after he had satisfied the law, and was no longer an involuntary prisoner.

They were afterwards taken to the court, and examined. They had no trial, neither were they allowed to meet their complainants face to face, but were condemned upon the evidence furnished by the depositions of two individuals, the stronger of the two documents being as follows:

"I, —— Cole, being in the market-place when Obadiah Holmes came from the whipping post, John Spur

came and met him pleasantly, laughing in his face, saying, 'Blessed be God for thee, brother;' and so did go
with him, laughing upon him, towards the prison,
which was very grievous to me to see him harden the
man in his sin, and showing much contempt of authority by that carriage, as if he had been unjustly punished, and had suffered as a rightous man under a tyrannical government. Deposed before the court the 5th
of the 7th month.   INCREASE NOWEL."

They were sentenced to receive ten lashes each, or
pay a fine of forty shillings. The latter they could
not conscientiously do. A Mr. Bendal, who was a friend
to Hazel, offered to pay his, but he refused saying, —
"I thank you for this offer of love; but I believe it
will be no acceptable service for any man to pay a
penny for me in this case." Yet, notwithstanding his
refusal, the court accepted the proffer, and gave him
his discharge. Hazel was upwards of sixty years of
age, and died soon after his release.*

Spur was kept in prison nearly a week, expecting
every day to be taken to the market square, tied to the
whipping post, and receive his ten lashes; but, without
his permission, some sympathizing friend paid his fine,
and secured his deliverance.

These persecutions were the means of attracting the
attention of many to the doctrines of the sufferers.
Sympathy elicited inquiry, and inquiry produced conviction. The sentiments of the Baptists spread. Many
were convinced of the scripturalness of their views of

---

* Benedict's History of the Baptists.

baptism, and desired to be buried with Christ in that beautiful and significant ordinance. Their desire could not be refused. The ordinance was administered repeatedly, though with the greatest privacy, for fear of prisons, fines, and scourgings.

———————

From following Letter, addressed to the Philadelphia Association, the reader will learn something of the cruel sufferings the Baptists of Massachusetts underwent, by being robbed of their lands and homes and very dead, to pay the salaries of Pedobaptist ministers and build parsonages and meeting houses, for them to live and preach in ! The Philadelphia Association, poor as they were, raised collections from all their churches and sent forward for the relief of their suffering brethren from time to time.

This was the character of affiliation the Pedobaptists had for Baptists. " Union protracted meetings " and exchange of pulpits were not desired by Pedobaptists *then,* nor did they then complain because Baptists did not invite them to their communion tables. Who but can admire the faithfulness and fortitude, in suffering cruel scourgings and the loss of all things for Christ's sake, displayed by our brethren in New England, only two hundred years ago? Should those times return, how few of us would be able to stand ?

Contents of Letter from New England, Relative to the Sufferings of Our Brethren at Ashfield, in Boston.

"The laws of this province were never intended to exempt the Baptists from paying towards building and repairing Presbyterian meeting houses, and making up Presbyterian ministers' salaries; for, besides other insufficiencies, they are all limited, both as to extent and duration. The first law extended only five miles round each Baptist meeting house; those without this circle had no relief, neither had they within; for, though it exempted their polls, it left their estates to the mercy of harpies, and their estates went to wreck. The Baptists sought a better law, and with great difficulty and waste of time and money, obtained it; but this was not universal. It extended not to any parish until a Presbyterian meeting house should be built, and a Presbyterian minister settled there; in consequence of which the Baptists have never been freed from the first and great expenses of their parishes, expenses equal to the current expenses of ten or twelve years. This is the present case of the people of Ashfield, which is a Baptist settlement. There were but five families of other denominations in the place when the Baptist Church was constituted; but those five, and a few more, have lately built a Presbyterian meeting house there, and settled an 'orthodox minister,' as they call him, which last cost them two hundred pounds ($1,000). To pay for both, they laid a tax on the land; and, as the Baptists are the most numerous, the greatest part fell to their share. The Presbyterians, in April last, demanded the money. The Baptists pleaded poverty, alleging that they had been twice driven from their plantations by Indians in the last war; that they were but new settlers, and had cleared but a few spots of land, and had not been able to build commodious dwelling houses. Their tyrants would not hear. Then the Baptists showed them the ingratitude of such conduct; for they had built a fort there at their own expense, and had maintained it for two years, and so had protected the interior Presbyterians, as well as their neighbors, who now rose up against them; that the Baptists to the westward had raised money to relieve Presbyterians, who had like them suffered by the Indians, and that it was cruel to take from them what the Indians had left! But nothing touched the hearts of these cruel people. Then the Baptists urged the law of the province, but were soon told that that law extended to no new parish till the meeting house and minister were paid for. Then the Baptists petitioned the General Court. Proceedings were stopped till further orders, and the poor people went home rejoicing, thinking their property safe; but had not all got home before said order came, and it was an order for the Presbyterians to proceed. Accordingly, in the month of April, they fell foul on the plantations, and not on skirts and corners, but on the cleared and improved spots, and so have mangled their estates and left them hardly any but a wilderness. They sold the house and garden of one man, and the young orchards, meadows, and cornfields of others; nay, they sold their dead, for they sold their graveyard. The orthodox (?)

minister was one of the purchasers. These spots amounted to three hundred and ninety-five acres, and have since been valued at £363 8s. ($1,815), but were sold for £35 10s. ($185). This was the first payment! Two more are coming, which will not leave them an inch of land at this rate. The Baptists waited on the assembly five times this year for relief, but were not heard, under pretense they did no business; but their enemies were heard and had their business done. At last the Baptists got together about a score of the members at Cambridge, and made their complaints known; but in general they were treated very superciliously. One of them spoke to this effect: '*The General Assembly have a right to do what they did, and if you don't like it, you may quit the place!*' But, alas! they must leave their land behind! These Presbyterians are not only supercilious in power, but mean and cruel in mastery. When they came together to mangle the estates of the Baptists, they diverted themselves with the tears and lamentations of the oppressed. One of them, whose name is Wells, stood up to preach a mock-sermon on the occasion; and among other things, used words to this effect: '*The Baptists, for refusing to pay an orthodox minister, shall be cut in pound pieces, and boiled for their fat, to grease the devil's carriage, etc.*"

The First Church in Providence

NOT THE

OLDEST BAPTIST CHURCH

IN AMERICA.

BY REV. S. ADLAM, D. D.

Late Pastor of the First Church in Newport, R. I.

EDITED BY J. R. GRAVES, LL. D.

———

PREFACE.

THE following pages owe their origin to a controversy going on since 1847, between the churches of Providence and Newport, as to priority of age.

Having, in the latter part of 1849, become the pastor of the latter church, I found it on several accounts necessary to satisfy my mind where the truth lay. I therefore resolved to make as thorough an examination of the subject as my means, opportunities and abilities would allow.

When I commenced my researches, I had no doubt but the truth was with the Providence church; and no one can be more surprised than was I, at the result to which I came. Nor could I be satisfied till I had repeated the investigation a second, a third, and a fourth time; and then showed the whole to gentlemen in whose judgment I placed great confidence, and heard from them that they could perceive no mistake.

For the sake of distinctness and ease of reference, I have divided what is said into chapters, and placed the subject discussed in each chapter at its head.

It was not till I had fully attained my result that I became acquainted with the manuscript referred to and

9   (129)

quoted in Chapter IV. The reading of that manuscript removed every suspicion that I had erred.

Should any reply, let me remind them, that the whole argument is contained in Chapter I. On that I rely; all the rest is intended to throw light upon and confirm that. Should I, therefore, be found to have erred (which I have earnestly endeavored to avoid) in any other part, my conclusions will remain untouched, unless that chapter be proved to be unsound.

I know of nothing that can be construed into a dis. respect of the Providence church, except it be the notice I have taken of their records; by which I mean the historic speech prefixed to them), and I have done no more than to show that *they can not be relied on as valid historical testimony.* No one now living is responsible for them. I suppose that if a sketch were at present to be made by some of the able members of that church, it would not only differ from that in the records, but would contradict them. Professor Knowles, in his life of Roger Williams, has pointed out some errors. Dr. Hague, in his Historical Discourse, has, on a most important and even vital point, as far as our discussion is concerned, opposed them. Staples, though he has done it with a gentle hand, has alluded to the misconception concerning Thomas Olney. Professor Gammell, a member of that church, and one of the committee to prepare the document read to the Association, in his life of Roger Williams, is at entire variance with the records concerning that distinguished man. Indeed, anyone who investigates facts for himself, will be convinced that on these records he can place no reliance as to what occurred before the time of Tillinghast; they are quite as likely to mislead as to guide. On this account, especially as our most popular historians rely on them as ultimate authority, I consider it my duty to show fully their inaccuracy.

It will soon be perceived that I write not for popular reading; but I appeal to men who can reason and reflect.

I wish to state distinctly that *one* question, and that alone, is here discussed. I enquire not who in America were the first persons baptized, where, or by whom; nor when any other church was constituted. The question is: "**Which** *is the oldest Baptist Church in America?* Is it the existing Newport, or the existing Providence church?" It is not for another, but for itself, the Providence church contends; the church in Newport does the same. Simple and obvious as this remark may appear, it is not without importance in this discussion.

In the Appendix I have more fully explained some things connected with the subject on which I have treated, but which it would not be well to consider in the body of the work.

What I have written I leave to calm, reflecting, impartial men ; their verdict will at last prevail, and to it I cheerfully submit.

NEWPORT, R. I.   S. A.

CHAPTER I.

*The Present Church in Providence a Seceder, or one from an
Older Church — Its True Date, and Founders.*

FOUR things are claimed by the church in Providence: that Roger Williams was its founder and first
pastor; that it was constituted in 1639; before any
other in the State; and that it is the oldest of the Baptists in America. All this, with the exception of Roger
Williams being its founder and first pastor, is inscribed
on its bell; and also on a tablet in its meeting-house.
Thousands, perhaps tens of thousands, have read this
tablet, and have supposed it to state undoubted facts.
But was it constituted in 1639? Was it the first in the
State? Is it the oldest of the Baptists in America?
And was Roger Williams its founder and first pastor?
Will a thorough examination sustain one of these
positions? Let the evidence that follows decide:

Staples, in his Annals of Providence, says: "There
were two Baptist Churches in Providence, as early as
1652; one of the six-principle and the other of the five-
principle Baptists. This appears from a manuscript
diary kept by John Comer, a Baptist preacher in Newport. It states that one of the members of the First
Baptist Church in Newport, "came to Providence, and
received imposition of hands from William Wickenden,
pastor of a church there lately separated from the
church under Thomas Olney, and that Mr. Wickenden and Mr. Gregory Dexter returned to Newport with

him; and that the same ordinance was administered to several others, who, in 1656, withdrew from the First Church in Newport, and formed a new church there, etc." Page 410.

Comer, in his manuscript, spells Wickenden's name, as it was probably pronounced, *Wigginton;* and his exact words are: "Mr. William Vaughn, finding a number of Baptists in the town of Providence, lately joined together in special church covenant, in the faith and practice, and under the inspection of Mr. William Wigginton, being heretofore members of the church under Mr. Thomas Olney, of that town, *i. e.*, Mr. William Vaughn went thither in the month of October, 1652, and submitted thereto (to the imposition of hands), upon which he returned to Newport, accompanied with Mr. William Wigginton and Mr. Gregory Dexter, etc."

Callender says: "About the year 1653 or '54, there was a division in the Baptist Church at Providence, about the right of laying on of hands, which some pleaded for as essentially necessary to church communion, and the others would leave indifferent. Hereupon they walked in two churches, one under C. Brown, Wickenden, etc., the other under Thomas Olney." Page 114.

Backus writes: "Thomas Olney, who had been a member of the Congregational Church in Salem, but left them and came to Providence in 1638, was the next pastor of this Baptist Church (founded by Roger Williams) until his death in 1682. But a division arose in the church in 1652, about the laying on of hands upon every member of the church after baptism. William Wickenden was a chief leader in that part of the church in Providence which held to laying on of hands upon each member, which they supposed to be intended in the sixth chapter of Hebrews; and he was an esteemed minister therein until he died in February 23, 1669." Vol. 3, p. 217. Again: "Thomas Olney, Senior, also died this year (1682). He was next to Mr. Williams in the pastoral office at Providence, and continued so to his death, over that part of the church who are called five-principle Baptists, in distinction from those who parted from their brethren, about the year 1653, under the leading of elder Wickenden, holding to the laying on of hands upon every church member." Vol. 1, p. 505.

Before I make any remarks on what has been adduced, I wish to show that the above statements are so far above contradiction, that they have been in their general features endorsed by the Providence church itself. Dr. Hague, late pastor of that church, in his "Historical Discourse," prepared with great care, and received with uncommon satisfaction and respect by his people, does not deny a single statement that Comer, or Callender, or Backus has made, but as far as he refers to this subject, harmonizes with them.

Speaking, in order, of the pastors of the church, when coming to Wickenden, page 95, he says: "With his name is connected our first intelligence of the rise of a controversy, which was long agitated in this town, and throughout the Commonwealth;" and then discussing the subject to which he alludes, viz, the laying on of hands, he quotes from Comer thus: "In 1652,

Rev. William Vaughn, of Newport, embraced this
view, and hearing that a church had been formed in
Providence on this basis, under the care of Rev. Mr.
Wickenden, he repaired thither, and having received
the rite himself, obtained the aid of Mr. Wickenden in
forming a similar body at Newport." Reviewing the
ministry of Dexter, first the associate, and then the
successor of Wickenden, Dr. Hague observes : "When
Mr. Vaughn visited Providence, in 1652, in order to
procure the aid of Mr. Wickenden in forming a church
which should hold the laying on of hands as a divine
ordinance, Mr. Dexter accompanied them to Newport,
and seems to have taken a part in that service; from
which we may infer that he had united with those who
had formed a separate church here under Mr. Wickenden." Page 98.

These statements prove that as early as 1652, '53, or
'54, two distinct Baptist Churches existed in Providence; that they were not only distinct bodies, but of
different orders; one a six, the other a five-principle
Baptist Church; that the six-principle was under the
care of Wickenden, Browne, and Dexter, while the five-
principle church was under the charge of Thomas
Olney.

They also prove that Olney's was the original, and
Wickenden's, Brown's, and Dexter's six-principle, the
seceding church.

Two things show that the existing is the seceding
church: *First* — Every writer, including the records,
mentions Brown, Wickenden, and Dexter as former
pastors of that church; *Second* — The present church,

from 1652 until 1770, was known only as a six-principle, while Olney's was the five-principle church.

From this it follows that the existing church in
Providence was not founded in 1639, but in 1652; it
was not the first in the State, for it came out from an
older church ; it is not the oldest of the Baptists in
America, for the Newport church was founded unquestionably eight years before; and so far from Roger
Williams being its founder and first pastor, he was in
England when it was founded; and thirteen years before he had ceased to be a Baptist.

It also follows that the time when Roger Williams
was baptized has nothing to do in determining the age
of the present church.

CHAPTER II.

Reliable Tradition Harmonizes with the Preceding View.

That no opportunity might be afforded for weaken-
ing the foregoing conclusion, I have kept strictly within the bounds of the highest documentary evidence;
I now add, that tradition of the most reliable character,
generally, if not universally, as far as the founders and
first pastors of the church are concerned, agrees with
the preceding view.

Stephen Hopkins, signer of the Declaration of Independence, grandson of Wickenden, uniformly affirmed
that Wickenden was the first elder of the existing
church, and asserted this in his "History of Providence," published in 1765. Moses Brown, that venerable nestor of Providence, as he is called by Knowles,

always held that his ancestor, Chad Brown, was the first elder of the Providence Baptist Church. John Angel, born in 1691, claimed the same honor for his grandfather, Gregory Dexter.

Nor is there any discrepancy in these claims. When the present venerable president of the Rhode Island Historical Society, John Howland, Esq., now over ninety years of age, told Moses Brown, with whom he was intimate sixty or seventy years ago, of the claims of Stephen Hopkins, which seemed to conflict with what he affirmed, Moses replied that "there was no contradiction, for they were probably both elders at the same time." A statement undoubtedly true; and the same may be said of Dexter, cotemporary with them both. The fact appears to be thus: C. Brown, Wickenden, and Dexter, in withdrawing from Olney's and setting up the present church, labored for awhile together. Chad Brown seems to have died first, Wickenden next, and Dexter, living to a great age, survived both. Under these circumstances it would be natural for the descendants of each, as they did, to claim for their progenitors the honor of being the first elders of that church.

Nor were the immediate descendants of these men the only ones of this opinion; in the early days of Providence it was the general, if not the universal belief.

Callender, in 1738, says: "The most ancient inhabitants now alive, some of them above eighty years old, who personally knew Mr. Williams, and were well acquainted with many of the original settlers, never heard that Mr. Williams formed the Baptist Church there, but always understood that Brown, Wickenden or Wigginton, Dexter, Olney, Tillinghast, etc., were the first founders of that church."*

This shows that the general opinion of Roger Williams being the founder and first pastor of that church, is a modern theory; the farther you go back the less generally is it believed; till coming to the most ancient times, to the men who knew Williams, they are such entire strangers to it, that they never heard that he formed the Baptist Church there. The first, and the second, and the third, and almost the fourth generation, must pass away before men can believe

---

*It is evident that Callender was not a little perplexed as to the relationship of Roger Williams to the Baptist cause in Providence. After stating in the text that it was said Williams became a Baptist, and formed a Baptist Church there, he adds, in a note: ''Since this was transcribed for the press, I find some reasons to suspect Mr. Williams did not form a church of the Anabaptists, and that he never joined with the Baptist Church there. Only that he allowed them to be nearest the Scriptural rule, and true primitive practice as to the mode and subject of baptism; but that he himself waited for new apostles," etc., and then follows the words I have quoted.

Morgan Edwards says: "I have one of the Century Sermons of Mr. Callender, with a *dele* upon this note, in his own handwriting." I have tried to find that sermon, that I may judge to what part of the note Callender referred; but I have not succeeded. What may we learn from that *dele?* That on some of the things referred to in this note, Callender changed his mind. What were they? Three distinct things are mentioned in the note: *First*—That Williams did not form a church (Baptist) in Providence; *Second*—That he never united with the church there; *Third*—That the most ancient inhabitants of that place, those who knew him, etc., never heard that he formed the church there, but that Brown, Wickenden, etc., were the founders of it."

Now it could not be the last of these items that Callender changed his mind upon; for this would be to convict himself of falsehood in originally making the statement. It must have been concerning the first and second items that the mind of Callender underwent a change; so that the *dele* does not affect the quotation I have made.

IN AMERICA. 139

that any others than Wickenden, Brown, etc., were
the founders of that church. Two other things deserve a passing notice: *First*—The college in 1770 was
built on its present site, "because it was the home lot
of Chad Brown, the first minister of the Baptist
Church;* and, *Second*—On the bell, and on the tablet,
Roger Williams is not mentioned as the founder of the
church. There is reason to believe that if an attempt
had been made to do it, it would have been stoutly
resisted by many in that day; and even by some of
the leading men of that house. Indeed there are
many of the most aged and well-informed men of
Providence at this day who contend that Roger Williams was not the founder of that church. All this
shows that tradition agrees with the documentary evidence before adduced, and yet all depends upon the
founders and first pastors of the church; for Williams'
church was founded in 1639, but Chad Brown's, Wickenden's and Dexter's not till 1652. The mistake lies in
the existing church, taking not its own, but another's date.

CHAPTER III.

*The Old Church, and the Relation of the Existing
Church to it.*

Having shown that the present separated from the
old five-principle church, in the year 1652, we feel some
interest to inquire concerning the fate of the original
body.

---

* Howland in *Knowles' Life of Roger Williams*, p. 174. Note.

Comer, Callender and Backus all agree that it remained under the care of Thomas Olney. As there is no difference of opinion upon this I shall only make one quotation, and that from Backus, already given: "Mr. Thomas Olney, Sr., died this year (1682). He was next to Mr. Williams in the pastoral office at Providence, and continued so to his death over that part of the church who are called five-principle Baptists, in distinction from those who parted from their brethren about the year 1653, under the leading of Elder Wickenden," etc. Vol. I, p. 505.

A melancholy interest invests the last notice we have of this ancient church. It continued till early in the last century, when it became extinct, leaving no records, and but few events in its history behind. The fullest information of it I have found is in a note by Callender on the one hundred and fifteenth page of his discourse. Speaking of this church he adds below: "This last continued till about twenty years, when, becoming destitute of an elder, the members were united with other churches; and further adds: "At present there is some prospect of their re-establishment in church order."

This was written in 1738. The church had then been extinct about twenty years; that is, it lost its visibility about 1718. Morgan Edwards says that the church under Olney continued till 1715. So that it continued after the division, in 1652, for more than sixty years, when, discouraged, they scattered, never to be united again. And thus passed away the original church, and the waves of time have almost obliterated its remembrance from the minds of men. Callender, indeed, thought that when he wrote that it might be re-established, and in this he would have rejoiced, as it would have afforded him a church that would hold communion with him and with the people under his care; but he was disappointed, and for more than one hundred and thirty years the old church in Providence is among the things that were.

After this review, what are we to understand Dr. Hague to refer to (p. 99) when he says that "the breach which then (1652) arose out of the controversy about laying on of hands as a divine right was afterwards healed?" How was it healed? By whom, and on what conditions? Did Wickenden's church ever give up its visibility, or merge itself into any other body? From the time of its formation, in 1652, till under Dr. Manning (1770), did it not continue strictly by profession, and in fact, a six-principle church? And when an attempt was made during his ministry to relax somewhat the stringency of the six principles, was it accomplished without great difficulty, and did it not cost a division? It was not till 1791 that the church clearly decided to admit as members those who did not hold the six principles; nor till 1808 that these sentiments were formally given up.

Dr. Hague's language seems to imply that the two churches came together and formed but one. No such an event can I trace in the history of either church. For more than sixty years they existed side by side, without once, so far as I know, having communed together. And as to the existing church, for more than a hundred years, it is not too much to say that it was in its communion among the strictest of the strict; nor do I know of an instance during that period of an attempt to relax the vigor of their practice without producing a reaction, and drawing the bounds of church fellowship within narrower limits.

It sometimes happens that when a church is reduced low, and is in distress, another will come to its aid; but the old Providence church, after having struggled for existence for more than sixty years, died unpitied and unwept. Has any one a right to take her date, and claim her founder? I trow not. The only place for the inscription: "This church was founded A. D. 1639," is the grave of Roger Williams' church.

CHAPTER IV.

Ancient History Sustains the Claims of the Newport Church.

We have found that the proper date of the Providence church is not 1639, but 1652, and thus it can not be the oldest of the Baptists in America. We now observe that ancient history ascribed this priority as to age to the church at Newport.

Comer, the first, and for the early history of our denomination, the most reliable of writers, ascribes distinctly and repeatedly this priority to the Newport church. He had formed the design, more than a hundred and twenty years ago, of writing the history of the American Baptists; and in that work, which he only lived to commence, but which embraces an account of this church, he says in one place: "That it is the first of the Baptist denomination." And closing his history of it, says: "Thus I have briefly given some account of the settlement and progress of the First Baptist Church on Rhode Island, in New England, and the first in America."

This was written about 1730; and to those acquainted with Comer, nothing need be said of the value of this testimony. For others I will extract from Benedict a brief notice of his character: "He began his education at Cambridge, but finished it at New Haven He bid fair to be one of the most eminent ministers of his day; his character was unspotted, and his talents respectable and popular; he had conceived the design of writing the history of the American Baptists, and for the purpose of forwarding it, traveled as far as Philadelphia, (a great undertaking at that day), opened a correspondence with persons in the different colonies, and also in England, Ireland, etc."

This excellent man, who took unwearied pains to procure for his history the most correct information, was especially distinguished for the extreme accuracy of his dates, was, when he wrote the above, himself a six-principle Baptist; was intimately acquainted with the church at Providence, and had advantages for knowing its early history that no other historian has since possessed.

From the way in which he asserts it, the priority of the Newport church must have been a universally conceded fact. He was careful to excess, not to record as certain, that on which any suspicion rested; and yet this father of American Baptist history, whose veracity

has never been questioned, with 1644 as the acknowledged date of the Newport church, states that in age it
is prior to any other Baptist Church in America. It is
true, and I was sorry to see it, some later hand has
added in a note: "Excepting that of Providence."
Who wrote this I will not say, but no one should
touch Comer's writings, unless he is a more reliable
witness than that painstaking and impartial man.

Besides his general carefulness, he was. when he
wrote the above, on the most favorable terms with the
Providence church, while a difficulty had occurred be·
tween him and the Newport church, which caused him
the most painful feelings. While pastor of that church,
he urged upon them the imposition of hands with con·
siderable earnestness, which brought on discussion and
alienation, till at last a separation took place, when he
immediately passed under the imposition of hands and
became the pastor of a six-principle church. It is true
that the breach was afterwards healed, and the account
of the reconciliation the church permitted him to make
—the last, of course, of his valuable entries in our
records. And, though the separation was unpleasant,
Comer's name is still held in affectionate remembrance
by the church.

Now, it was while suffering from the above cause,
when, if ever, he was under temptation to suppress the
truth, that he most unhesitatingly affirms the Newport
church to be the first of the Baptists in America. He
was, however, above temptation to pervert on any
occasion the truth; and he must have known that
what he wrote was not only correct, but it was at that

time generally, if not universally, acknowledged to be so. He makes no exception to this remark, and he was too well acquainted with the history of the church in Providence to except that—for he well knew that it was not formed till 1652, eight years after that in Newport.

Should it appear strange that, if the claim of the Newport church was well founded, it should suffer it to be taken away, and not reclaimed till within a few years, the solution is plain?

Soon after the church at Providence had affixed to itself a wrong date, the war of the Revolution came on; and in that great national crisis no place suffered more than Newport. It was early taken, and long held by the British forces; the property of its citizens was taken; its commerce crippled; its merchants, distinguished for enterprise, intelligence, and wealth, fled, never to return. Amid the general distress, none suffered more than the First Church. Its pastor was forced from his charge; its members were scattered; its sanctuary, dedicated by the saintly and talented Callender, and where, with so much sweetness, he had preached the Gospel, was seized, desecrated, mangled, for the use of the British soldiers—and when, at last, a few returned and looked on the desolation of their beloved Zion, they wept; they were poor, long had they to struggle even for existence, and probably knew not, or thought not, that their birthright was about to be taken from them. A series of events occurred that left not the church at liberty to put forth her appeal for that distinction which she so fairly deserves, and which at

10

first, we doubt not, every church freely accorded to her.
But still the members felt, and with them the island at
large, an assurance that nothing could shake, that it
was this church which first in America raised aloft the
Baptist standard, and that its founder and first members toiled and suffered, and knew what prison walls
and scourges were, before our sister church at Providence had breathed the breath of life. Nor did they
doubt but at last they could make it appear. Dates
they knew somewhere or somehow were wrong, and
suspected their own ; and while looking over the family title deeds to verify or correct theirs, they found
that in some way or other their sister had mistaken hers.

CHAPTER V

Source of Prevailing Errors — Hopkins—Church Records.

The church at Providence never has had any creed,
or any covenant; till the year 1700 it had no meeting
house, but in fine weather worshiped in a grove, and
when inclement, in private houses; nor till the year
1775 had it any regular records. Can we be surprised
that in tracing the history of such a body, a hundred
years after its origin, unless ancient writers are care-
fully studied, that material errors will be made?

Those who first in modern times (I mean within the
last hundred years) undertook to write concerning the
Providence church, though excellent men in other respects, were sadly unqualified for their work. The days
of Comer and of Callender had passed away. It seems

as though between 1760 and 1780 Baptist history in
Providence underwent a total eclipse. Different persons
and churches were strangely jumbled together; and as
the result of this confusion, the present church assumed
a position it did not before hold, and to which, by
right, it has not the shadow of a claim.

Stephen Hopkins, in 1765, is the first I can discover
who assigned to the present church a date earlier than
1652; and he endeavored to unite the impossible conditions of the true founder and this early date. He
claimed for his grandfather, Wickenden, the honor of
being its first elder, and in this he was correct · but he
committed a grave mistake in attributing by implication to Wickenden the baptism of those who were baptized in 1638 or 1639 — an honor that belongs indisputably to Roger Williams. Succeeding writers saw
that Hopkins' early date must be given up, if Wickenden were retained as the first pastor: and, themselves
misled, they adopted the erroneous date, and pushing
aside its true founder, Hopkins' grandfather, they put
Roger Williams in his place. And thus by two errors,
one built on the other, Roger Williams is made the
founder and first pastor of a church with which we
know not that he ever worshiped, or had the least sympathy, and which did not even begin to exist till thirteen years after he had ceased to be a Baptist; and that
church has been led to assume a distinction which
belongs to another.

It would be unnecessary to point out in detail the
errors of each writer. after Stephen Hopkins The way
is the same in all. They confound Roger Williams'

with the present church, and thus carry back its date to thirteen years before it began to exist.

The errors and misconceptions arising therefrom are seen in a striking manner in the Records of the Providence church. And as these records have, by being published, become public property, as they are appealed to by our most widely read historians, and as upon them ultimately must rest the claims of the Providence church, we shall examine what reliance can be placed upon them.

That the author or compiler of these records was honest, I doubt not; but that he possessed the information, the ability for patient research, and the discrimination necessary for a historian, I can not believe. Take as examples the following serious errors:

"So little did he know of the true origin of that church, whose history for more than a hundred years he undertook to compile, that he not only makes Roger Williams to be its first pastor, but represents that he was its pastor about four years, when it is well known that he was a Baptist only four months! After he left the Baptists, Roger Williams lived forty-three years, and yet from these records you would not suspect but he was a Baptist to the day of his death. After being a Baptist four months, Williams denied that there was any true ministry, or any true church, and yet in these records he is represented at the end of four years as resigning his pastoral office to Brown and Wickenden!"

This specimen would be enough to satisfy any who were seeking the truth; but proceed, and mark the short but very inaccurate account of Thomas Olney.

That I may not be charged with unfairness or misrepresentation, I will quote it entire:

"Rev. Thomas Olney succeeded (Gregory Dexter) to the pastoral office. He was born at Hertford, in England, about the year 1631, and came to Providence in 1654; but when baptized or ordained is not known. He was the chief who made a division about laying on of hands. He and others withdrew, and formed a separate church, but it continued only a short time. He died June 11, 1722, and was buried in his own field."

Difficult would it be in the same amount of language to find so much misconception and error as here. Never should Thomas Olney, to whom justice has not yet been done, have been spoken of thus. The writer, doubtless, intended to be correct; but so little did he know of history, that he confounded two individuals, probably father and son, together. If he alludes to the son, then it was not in his, but in his father's day that the division occurred. If he alludes to the father, then he died, not in 1722, but forty years before, in 1682. This confusion of persons and dates would invalidate any testimony. But this is not all. Olney is placed as the successor of Brown, Wickenden, and Dexter. In the ministry he preceded them all; and never was pastor of the church which they set up. The records say that he was the chief who made the division, and that he and others with him withdrew and formed a separate church. It was Wickenden and his associates that went off; and even Dr. Hague says it was they who formed the separate church. The records say that he came to Providence in 1654; he was town treasurer of that place in 1639. But I forbear. It may be said that the records speak not of the father, but of the son. Then where is the evidence that the Olney who died in 1722 was pastor of Wickenden's church after Dexter's death; that he made a division about the laying on of hands; that he withdrew and formed a separate church? Is there a single ancient writer that has recorded it, or alluded to it? And if the son be alluded to, where, in giving an account of Baptist ministers in Providence, is the father alluded to — that ancient man in whose day a division did take place; and who saw, in 1652, his church receive such a wound, that after sixty years struggling for existence, it at last expired?

Look also at Chad Brown; he is made pastor of the church ten years before it began to exist!

But I will pursue this subject no farther. What is the value of records like these? And yet it is by these records, and documents like them, that the Providence church carries its date back to 1639, claims to be the first in the State, and the oldest of the Baptists in America.

We have seen in Chapter I. how completely history refutes the claims of that church; but, if possible, the records on which they rely refute them more completely still.

Thinking men will be ready to doubt, if records so prepared are the highest authority on which grave historians rest in giving an account of that church, and on which that church's peculiar claims depend. But hear what Benedict, who well knows the facts in

1848, says. Closing, in his history, his notice of this church, he observes, "My present historical details are taken partly from my first volume, and partly from Hague's Historical Discourse, delivered in 1839, at the expiration of two hundred years from the founding of the church. *But the church records are the only source of information to us all!*" Is it so? Is it by records like these that the ancient, and in her early days, when she stood all alone, the suffering church at Newport, is to be disrobed of her distinction, and another that did not begin to be, till she had endured fine, imprisonment, and scourging for the Baptist cause, to receive it? Is it by such records that the church in Providence claims to be the first in the State, and the oldest of the Baptists in America? Then let the present generation and let posterity know on what these claims rest. The claims and the records are of equal value — they are both alike.

CHAPTER VI.

Conclusion.

My investigation is brought to a close. I have pursued it fearlessly; I hope fairly. The time has fully come when the errors that have produced a most disastrous effect upon the general history of our denomination, should, with a faithful but a truthful hand, be laid bare. Ancient authors should again be heard, and modern misconception and confusion of thought should resign their rule. Little, when I commenced my inquiries, did I anticipate my result. I expected that with great plainness of speech (the only thing allow-

able in a discussion where truth is at stake), I should
have to show to the Newport church the unsoundness
of its claims. I should not have spoken as I have, had
I not surveyed, as far as I could, the entire field. I
am earnest, but it is the earnestness of conviction;
nor have I ventured upon a single position without
probing it to the foundation and inquiring if it can be
successfully assailed. And happy am I, that I have
been speaking of a church that has so many members,
able, if I have committed mistakes, to detect and ex-
pose them. If I have not been thorough in my examination—if I have misquoted or misrepresented any
author—or if I have passed by or suppressed any ancient
document, or kept back any circumstances that would
place this subject in a different light, they will know
it. If, in 1652, there were not in Providence two
churches — one a five, and the other a six-principle
church—if theirs was not the seceding and Olney's the
original body — if the old church did not, about the
year 1715, die out — if tradition does not mention
Brown, Wickenden, etc., and not Roger Williams, as
the founders of the present church — if there is not,
even to this day, in Providence, among some of its
oldest and best informed inhabitants, a conviction
which nothing can shake, that Roger Williams was not
the founder of their church— if the earliest history does
not unhesitatingly assign priority of age to the church
at Newport— if the records of the Providence church
can be vindicated — if the date 1639 does not belong
to another body and not to themselves—and if all their
claims are not based on misconception and error, they

can make it appear. The documents on which I have
relied are at their command, within the sound of their
bell, if not immediately under their hand. But if they
can not disprove what I have said (and I think they
can not), then, if there be a single truth on which we
can rely, the Providence church was not founded in
1639, but in 1652; it was not the first in the State, nor
is it the oldest in America; and if there is a church to
which that distinction belongs of right, and fairly
beyond dispute, it is the Newport church.

CHAPTER VII.

Which was the First Baptist Church Established in America?

It will be seen that I have not claimed in the preceding discussion all that belongs to the Newport
church. It is not only, according to history, the oldest,
but also the First Baptist Church established in America. My reason for not insisting on this before was
the desire to keep one question steadily before the
mind; and that being settled, we could better proceed.
The question as to which is the oldest church having
been discussed, we can now attend to that at the head
of this chapter.

I can see no evidence that Roger Williams, in the
ordinary acceptation of the term, established a Baptist
Church in Providence. When he was baptized, he
doubtless intended to do this; but he was not the man,
and the attempt was a failure.

That the church which he began to collect fell to

pieces soon after he left them, is what we should expect; and is, as far as I can learn, the uniform declaration of writers of that day.

It has been the practice with Baptist writers to put this down as Pedobaptist misrepresentation; but on what ground I know not. They gave a true statement of him and his views, viz: That after being a Baptist four months, he renounced his baptism, the ministry, and the church, believing that there was no true visible church, no true ministry, nor any one that had a right to administer ordinances. If they speak truthfully concerning him, why should they be doubted when they speak concerning his church? If they thought his church did exist, they must have known that it would be a standing monument, known and read of all men, against their declarations.

Look at the circumstances also. Here was a church gathered by one, in every respect their leader, the only learned man among them, and whose influence over them at that time was immense; as soon as he was baptized, and had baptized them, he began to doubt the propriety of the act. And in the space of four months had fully made up his mind that there was neither a true ministry nor true church on earth; a conviction so strong that he never wavered in it for the forty-three years of his after life. What could be expected of these brethren who had not the light which we enjoy, but were just emerging out of darkness, themselves, as well as their leader, having been bred in the belief that a regular succession from the apostles downward was necessary to a true church and a true

ministry? To persuade us that they would, under
these circumstances, continue together as a church,
requires the most undoubted evidence—but instead of
this, the evidence is the contrary way.

The perplexity into which these brethren were
thrown for want of a valid administrator is seen by an
account introduced by Backus. They heard that the
Queen of Hungary, or some in those parts, had a register of a regular succession from the apostles, and they
thought of sending Mr. Thomas Olney into that country for it.

It is well that a Baptist writer has recorded this;
for of all the strange things recorded by Pedobaptists
concerning our brethren at Providence, this is the
strangest of all. Send to the Queen of Hungary, or
some in those parts, for a register of a regular succession from the apostles, that they might be able to
establish a valid Baptist Church! It shows how much
Roger Williams had terrified them as to succession. I
do not blame them. They were simple-hearted, honest,
conscientious men, willing to do all they could, and to
go anywhere, so that they may obey the Savior; but
they were fettered with what does not trouble us, with
the idea of "apostolic succession." And if any are dis-
posed to smile at these unlettered Baptists, let them
remember that in 1850 there are thousands of learned
men bound hand and foot, and who scarcely dare think
their own thoughts, on account of the "succession."
These Providence Baptists showed not a little vigor in
emancipating themselves as soon as they did. But it is
too much to believe, without strong evidence, that they

could stand the shock of Williams' arguments, so as to keep as a church together. It must have appeared like presumption for them, all lay brethren, to attempt to administer ordinances, when Williams, their pastor, declared that no man, without a special commission from heaven, had a right to do it. And as to Williams ordaining any one during the four months that he was a Baptist, and while his mind was so distressingly agitated, it is too absurd for a moment to believe.

There is one writer whose testimony is of the highest value on this subject. I allude to Thomas Lechford, who was in New England from 1637 till about August, 1641; and among other places he visited Providence, somewhere, I judge, about the close of 1640, or the beginning of 1641. He inquired with great diligence into the ecclesiastical affairs of the country, and gave a faithful account. Against the Baptists he had no special prejudices more than against the Congregationalists, for he was an Episcopalian; but whatever were his own convictions, I have gained in many respects a more exact view of New England during these four years from him than from any other person. When speaking of Providence he says: " At Providence, which is twenty miles from the said island (Rhode Island, which he had also visited), lives Master *Williams*, and his company, of divers opinions— most are Anabaptists. They hold there is no true visible church in the *Bay*, nor in the world, nor any true ministry."

Mark this account. It is from an eye witness, about a year and a half after Williams renounced baptism, churches, ministry, and all. It is from a discriminating writer. He does not say that all were Anabaptists, but that most were. He has not a word of reproach to utter against them or Williams. He tells things just as they are. Providence at that time also was small, and had but few inhabitants, so that he could easily become acquainted with them. Now the opinion of these Anabaptists at Providence was that there was no true visible church in the Bay, nor in the world, nor any true ministry. Of course they could not have had a church. Lechford, then a purely unexceptionable witness, confirms what others have said, that Roger Williams' church, after he left them, crumbled to pieces.

We have seen from Callender that, in his day, the oldest men, those who knew him, and were well acquainted with many of the most ancient inhabitants, never heard that Roger Williams was the founder of the Baptist Church there—so soon and so completely was that church dissolved.*

When Olney's church was formed I can not tell; but

---

* Callender's opinion may be quoted against this view: but we have seen under the foregoing note that Callender himself was perplexed concerning the relations of Williams to the Baptist cause. He opposes the view of Neale that the church of Williams crumbled to pieces, because a few years after a flourishing Baptist Church was there. As Callender, however, had, while transcribing his sermon for the press, changed his mind about Williams forming a church in Providence, he must have supposed that finding a flourishing Baptist Church there some years afterwards might as well be accounted for on the supposition that it was formed by Brown, Wickenden, etc., as by its being originally formed by Williams, and having stood while he, its foundation, fell—fell as a Baptist to rise no more. This latter view is undoubtedly correct. Nor have we any evidence that Callender, on this point, went back to the views of the text.

as Comer, dating the Newport church no further back than 1644, says it was the first of the Baptist denomination in America, Olney's church could not have been formed till after that period.

I think it could not have been formed till about the year 1650. My reasons are, I find no trace of a Baptist Church in Providence after the failure of Roger Williams till after that year. The first intimation of a church there, I find in the fall of 1651, when Holmes, after being scourged in Boston, returning home, says: "The brethren of our town (Rehoboth) and Providence having taken pains to meet me four miles in the woods we rejoiced together." This occurred in September, 1651. Even this notice does not prove that a church existed in Providence at that time, for he speaks simply of the brethren of Rehoboth and of Providence. In Rehoboth there was no Baptist Church, for Holmes and his brethren then belonged to the church at Newport; and we are not certain their brethren at Providence were gathered into a distinct church any more than were those of Rehoboth.

That it was as late as I have fixed also appears from another circumstance. I have not been able to find a single individual out of Providence who united with that church till after 1652; but every Baptist up to that time known to belong to a church, live where he may, belonged to the church at Newport. We know that in the year 1651 the Newport church had members in Lynn and Rehoboth, in Massachusetts; and that persons came from Connecticut to unite with it. The case of the brethren in Rehoboth is peculiarly in point. In 1650 they left the Congregationalists and became

Baptists. If at that time a church had existed in Providence, a neighboring town, how natural they should unite with it, so near and easy of access, and not go all the way down to Newport to unite with the church there. The only way to account for this is, that there was no church at Providence, and no administrator there to whom they could apply.

It may be said that the number of Baptists whose names are recorded at that early date is few. Granted, but how does it happen that all those in another State, from thirty to near a hundred miles from Newport, should belong to that church, and not one of them to Providence?

Shall I mention one or two circumstances more? Before 1652 some work had been performed in Massachusetts—the Baptist standard had been lifted up on its high places. Enough had been done by that time to lay the foundation for a Baptist Church in Boston, in 1665, and to lead the first President of Cambridge College so to look at the subject as ultimately to become a Baptist. Who did that work? The members of the Newport church. Some little suffering before that time had been endured for the Baptist cause. Baptists had been fined, imprisoned, scourged. Newport, and she alone, was the suffering church. And what, with the exception of Roger Williams' attempt and failure, to the year 1652, and even beyond it, is nearly the entire history of our denomination, but the history of that same church?

How can we account for this but on the supposition that the church of Newport was the first Baptist

Church established in America? If before 1644 a church did exist in Providence, how is it that neither friend nor foe has noticed her; that every Baptist passed her by, even her nearest neighbors, and hurried down to Newport? How is it that for so many years she did nothing, suffered nothing, that no historian has been able to glean from her a line, find that not a single sign of vitality has been, up to that period, recorded of her?

The only conclusion to which we can come is that the Newport church is not only older than the present church at Providence, but older than any from which it came off.

Williams, indeed, touched the Baptist standard, but ere he raised it his hands trembled, and it fell. It was seized by a steadier hand; at Newport it was raised, and far and near they came to it; it was carried into the heart of Massachusetts, and a work was commenced which till the last setting of the sun shall never cease; and this before we have any evidence that a church in Providence had begun to be.

Among the evils that have resulted from the wrong date of the Providence church has been the prominence given to Roger Williams. It is greatly to be regretted that it ever entered into the mind of any one to make him, in America, the founder of our denomination. In no sense was he so. Well would it be for Baptists, and for Williams himself, could his short and fitful attempt to become a Baptist be obliterated from the minds of men. A man only four months a Baptist and then renouncing his baptism forever, to be lauded and magnified as the founder of the Baptist denomination in the New World! As a leader in civil and religious liberty, I do him homage; as a Baptist, I owe him nothing.

There is another name, long, too long, concealed by Williams being placed before him, who will in after times be regarded with unmingled affection and respect, as the true founder of the Baptist cause in this country. That orb of purest lustre will yet shine forth, and Baptists, whether they regard his spotless character, his talents, his learning, the services he rendered, the urbanity and the modesty that distinguished him, will mention JOHN CLARKE as the real founder of our denomination in America. And when Baptist history is better understood than it is at present, every one, pointing to that venerable church which, on one of earth's loveliest spots, he established, will say : " *This is the mother of us all!* " *

---

* The matter of the formation of the First Baptist Church was brought before the Warren Association at its meeting in 1847, and at the annual meeting of the association in 1848 the following votes were passed by that body:

" *First*—That the date of 1638, inserted under the name of the First Baptist Church in Newport, contained in the tabular *estimate* in the minutes of last year, be stricken out and the date (1644) be inserted, as in the minutes of the years preceding.

" *Second*—That a committee, consisting of T. C. Jameson, J. P. Tustin, and Levi Hale, be appointed to inquire into the evidence as to the date of the First Baptist Church in Newport, with instructions to report at the next session of the association."

This committee reported in 1849, that they are of the opinion that this church was formed certainly before the 1st of May, 1639, and probably on the 7th of March, 1638.

This called out a review of the fore-named report by a committee of the First Baptist Church in Providence, whose report is dated August 22, 1850, which led Rev. S. Adlam, who had just settled over the First Church in Newport, to make a thorough investigation of the matter, which resulted in his book upon the First Baptist Church in Providence.

It was expected that this book would call out a reply from some one of the First Church in Providence, as there were several very able members of that church professors in Brown University, but as no reply came, Mr. Adlam asked one of their ablest men (I am reliably informed) when his little book was to be answered? He replied : " **It is unanswerable.**"

ASA HILDRETH,
Clerk of First Church, Newport, R. I.

APPENDIX.

BY J. R. GRAVES.

In every department of Baptist ministry I confess myself greatly interested. Its importance is only next to the Bible. Indeed, by far the largest portion of the New Testament is the history of the early churches. It is a matter of no little gratification to me that much pertaining to the history of Baptists is yearly clearing up, and their sole claims to an apostolic origin more and more satisfactorily vindicated.

The foregoing historical paper by Elder S. Adlam, I read several years since with very great interest and satisfaction, and a correspondence followed.

In the course of my reading I met with the following statements in Crosby, and in the history of the Philadelphia Association, to which I called the attention of Elder Adlam:

" *When the First Church in Newport was one hundred years old, in* 1738, *Mr. John Callender, their minister, delivered and published a sermon on the occasion.*" Note on page 455.

This is Cotton Mather's testimony as to the perpetuity of Williams' informal society. If it was in existence when Mather wrote, he well knew it. If it dissolved when Williams left it, and repudiated it as a scriptural church, he knew it; and he says it "*came to nothing,*" there was nothing left for even Mather to reproach, and Mather died in 1727-8:

"One Roger Williams, a preacher, arrived in New England about the year 1630; was first an assistant in the church of Salem, and afterwards pastor. This man, a difference happening between the government and him, caused a great deal of trouble and vexation. At length the magistrates passed the sentence of banishment upon him, upon which he removed with a few of his own sect and settled at a place called Providence. 'There they proceeded,' says Mr. Mather, 'not only unto the gathering of a thing like a church, but unto the renouncing of their infant baptism.' After this, he says, he turned *Seeker* and *Familist*, and the church came to nothing." *

In reply to this letter, in which I inquired if his historical sketch had ever been successfully assailed— its dates and facts questioned — also, if the articles of faith were in existence upon which the Newport church was constituted — I received the following, parts of which are for one reason important here, as they will be interesting:

NEPWORT, R. I., May 4, 1857.

Rev. J. R. Graves.

MY DEAR BRO.: — In my last I intimated that I hoped, notwithstanding the demands made on my energies by the church, I should be able to complete the work I have begun. That a history of the early Baptists of America is desirable, all who have paid any

---

* See Mather's Ecclesiastical History of New England, p. 7, quoted from Crosby, Vol. I, p. 117.

attention to the subject must allow. Nothing that I have seen is correct, and what information is given, is presented in so involved and perplexed a way as to deprive it of all interest and power. Besides, the points in which they were in advance of all other Christians, and which, therefore, must constitute their peculiar claim to our attention, has been most imperfectly set forth. On these accounts I think it is due to the cause of truth that something more should be done than has been hitherto attempted to place the early history of our denomination in this country in a clear light; and I know of no place where it can be better done than in Newport. I have, therefore, kept this constantly in view, gleaning every fact that has come under my notice, and putting it, as well as I can, in its proper place, so as at last to make a correct and intelligible whole, showing not only the events as they transpired, but also the principles which they brought forth, and which bind them in unity together. With engagements like mine, such a process must be slow, but I hope an opportunity may occur when I may complete, however imperfectly, what is so desirable to be done.

Yourself would have the first offer of the work when it is in a fit state to go out of my own hands. Your interest in the subject and your generous course toward myself demand this; and I hope I am not insensible of kindness, come from what source it may. * * *

Respecting my pamphlet, I would observe that I see no reason to alter a single statement, or the general conclusion to which, in it, I came. Again and again have I reviewed it. I know that the same has been done by those who are able to detect errors, if any there be in it, and whose feelings would prompt them to do it. I have not a particle of doubt but the result will at length, however slowly, be placed among the indubitable facts ot history. My mind is entirely at rest as far as that is concerned.

You will recollect that my object in that pamphlet was to show that the first church in Providence was not constituted, as it professes to have been, in 1639, but in 1652 ; and that instead of being the first church constituted in Providence, it came out in the year just mentioned from an older church in that place; and, still more, that instead of having been originally a regular Baptist Church, it left the regular Baptist Church in Providence, its members having embraced the principles of the six-principle Baptists.

When I wrote that pamphlet I said nothing of *the real age of the First Baptist Church in Newport;* the age *generally* assigned to it answering my purpose as well as an earlier date. *I did not, however, concede that the correct date of the Newport church was, as is generally stated,* 1644, *for I have reasons for thinking that its proper date was some years earlier.* But as this was not the subject I undertook to discuss I passed it by. It was in reference to my views, unexpressed, that I stated on page 153: "I wish to state distinctly that one question, and that alone, is here discussed. I inquire not who in America were the first persons baptized, where, or by whom ; nor where any other church was constituted. The question is, ' Which is the oldest Baptist Church in America? Is it the existing Newport or the existing Providence church?'" etc.

You ask the question, "How can the centenary sermon of Callender, preached in 1738, agree with the date 1644, that has been assigned to the Newport church?"

After all the investigations I have made, I have come to the conclusion that the true date of the Newport church is 1638, and that any other is altogether arbitrary.

My reasons for these views are the following: We know that in the year 1638 a church was formed on the island, and Dr. Clarke became its pastor, and we have no information that that church ever became extinct.* On the island there is no allusion to such an event in any record, nor does tradition ever speak of our church but as the original church on the island. Other churches came out from us, we from no other. But in all the discussions that are recorded to have taken place baptism never had a place. Now it would be next to impossible that the pastor of the original church should have changed his sentiments on the subject of baptism, and should have been baptized himself without it having caused some discussion on the subject. But, instead of this, not a word can we find in any record, nor the least allusion in any tradition, that Dr. Clarke ever changed, on the island, his views concerning baptism, or that he was ever in this country baptized. The only way to account for this is, that

---

* See a brief history of that church, and list of its pastors, that concludes this book, for a proof of its continuance.—EDITOR.

no such event ever occurred; that he came to this country as a Baptist, and that as such he was known from the beginning. Another evidence, at least of strong probability, that the church on the island was, as explained, Baptist from the beginning, is seen in the fact that no Pedobaptist Church existed on the island till near sixty years after its settlement; and we never have heard of a single child that was baptized on the island for that time. Can we now suppose that, if the church was originally Pedobaptist, this would have been the case? Would not the Pedobaptist portion, when Clarke was baptized, have continued the old organization, and have had at least occasional preaching of that order till they had strength sufficient to have a settled pastor among them? Taking now all into view, I can not conceive it at all probable that Clarke was a Pedobaptist and the pastor of a Pedobaptist Church, and that yet he should change his sentiments, and Pedobaptism be overturned for near sixty years, and yet this done so quietly that it caused no feeling, no discussion—and this, too, among men intelligent and able, as well as ready, to defend their sentiments with earnestness, caring little for peace when they thought truth was at stake! Did such a thing ever occur? Is it probable? Is it possible? If not, then we must conclude that the church has always been what it has been universally, on the island, conceded to have been—a Baptist Church from the beginning. That beginning was in 1638.

To throw still more light on the subject, I observe that the results were just what may have been expected

in the case if matters were as I have supposed. Most
of those that came to the island were undoubtedly
Pedobaptists. But they had been terribly persecuted
by the Pedobaptist ministers of Massachusetts, while
for Clarke, however much they may differ from him,
they had the greatest respect; and in his honesty they
placed the most unlimited confidence. They would
listen to him while he would show the unscriptural
character of Pedobaptism, and were, there is every
reason to believe, convinced by him: but at that time
the Quaker doctrine concerning ordinances was introduced into the island; and as many of the heathen,
when their former sentiments have been proved false,
fly not to the truth, but to infidelity, so those Pedobaptists, finding that Pedobaptism was unscriptural,
very readily fell into the views then spread on the
island, with amazing zeal, that all ordinances were
done away, and that spiritual worship was the only
thing acceptable in the sight of God. In other words,
they became Quakers. And so we find for *near sixty
years*, the island was divided between Baptist and Quakers; the Quakers forming by far the largest number,
and numbering in their ranks the leading men that
came out of Massachusetts. All this is perfectly reasonable on the supposition that Clarke commenced his
labors as a Baptist on the island, and thus undermined
Pedobaptism, but most unaccountable on the supposition that he was a Pedobaptist, and that the church
which he served was a Pedobaptist church.

I have stated that I thought he was acquainted with,
if not ecclesiastically connected with, the church in

London, under the care of Spilsbury, Kiffin, etc. My
reason for this opinion is, that when Obadiah Holmes
wrote an account of his sufferings in Massachusetts, in
the year 1651, he sent it to "the well-beloved brethren,
John Spilsbury, William Kiffin, and the rest that in
London who stand fast in that faith, and continue to
walk steadfastly in that order of the gospel which was
once delivered to the saints by Jesus Christ." And as
he was not a Baptist in England, but was baptized by
Dr. Clarke, in this country, I think it probable he
became acquainted with these brethren by Dr. Clarke;
and as Dr. Clarke was acquainted with them, I think
it probable his acquaintance must have been formed
with them in England; and to have been acquainted
with them, under the then existing circumstances, was
nearly the same as to be ecclesiastically connected with
them.

But while I think, for the above reasons, that 1638
is the correct date of the church, still this is not necessary in order to prove that ours is the oldest Baptist
Church in America; for as the first in Providence was
not constituted till 1652, if our church did not exist till
1644 we are the older by eight years.

Touching the faith of John Clarke: In 1651, among
the things he undertook to defend as a part of his faith,
before the ministers and magistrates of Massachusetts,
but which they evaded, we find after he had proved
"that baptism or dipping in water is one of the com-
mands of this Lord Jesus Christ," and "that a visible
believer or disciple of Christ Jesus, (that is, one that
manifesteth repentance towards God, and faith in Jesus

Christ), is the only person that is to be baptized with that visible baptism or dipping of Jesus Christ in water;" he then adds, "and also the only person that is to walk in the visible order of His house," are such baptized persons.   And as you may wish to have his own words on this subject, I will transcribe them:

"That he" [the immersed believer] "is the only person that is to enter into, and walk in the visible order of His house, will evidently appear, if the order in which our Lord left His house when He went to His Father to receive His kingdom be duly considered; for in His last will and testament we shall find it thus recorded: when our Lord was about to be gone, He gave order unto His apostles, whom He made stewards in His house of the mysteries of God, to make Him disciples of all nations; and that such as were so made should then be baptized, and so visibly planted into Christ, and put on Christ; and having so received Him, should walk in Him, observing all things whatsoever He had commanded; the first thing whereof, as touching order, was to be added or joined one to another in the fellowship of the gospel, by a mutual professed subjection to the sceptre of Christ, and being a company thus called out of the world, from worldly vanities and worldly worships, after Christ Jesus the Lord, (which is the proper English of these words, the Church of Christ, and is in other terms called the household of faith,) should steadfastly continue together in the apostle's doctrine, *sci.*, the consolation, reproof, and instruction thereof; in fellowship; *sci.*, mutual support both inward and outward; in breaking of bread, thereby remembering the death of our Lord, whose soul was made an offering for sin, as His flesh is meat indeed, and His blood drink indeed, by the help of the Spirit, to nourish our souls and spirits up unto eternal life; and in prayer, one with and for another.   And that

this is the absolute order which the Lord hath appointed
in His last will and testament, doth evidently appear
both by His own precept and command, and by the
practice of such as first trusted in Him; and if so, then
neither infants of days, nor yet such as profess themselves to be believers in Jesus, but refuse as a manifestation thereof, according to the practice of such as first
trusted in Christ, to yield up themselves to be planted
into the death, burial, and resurrection of Christ, and
so visibly to put on Christ, as did the Christians of old;
I say such have no visible right to enter into, or walk
in the order of the gospel of Christ; and to conclude
the point, the argument stands thus: They, and
they only, have visible right to enter into and walk
in the visible order of Christ's house, and so to wait
for His coming, whom Christ Jesus, Himself being
the Lord of the house, hath appointed, and His apostles,
being His stewards, have approved of. But such as
first have been made disciples or scholars of Jesus, and
believers in Christ, and afterwards have been baptized
or dipped, and thereby visibly and lively planted into
the death, burial, and resurrection of Christ, are they,
and they only, whom Christ hath appointed, and the
apostles have approved of. See His commission; peruse
their practice: *ergo,* They, and they only, have visible
right to enter into and walk in the order of Christ's
house, and *so to wait for His coming the second time, in the
form of a King with His glorious kingdom, according to
promise.* See for a farther confirmation of the last clause,
in the 1st Epistle to the Corinthians, i, 7: 1 Thes. i,
10: 2 Thes. iii, 5." *

This, probably, is as far as any would go; and it
shows how thoroughly he had imbibed Baptist senti-

* Mark: Clarke was a premillennialist, as were all orthodox Baptists of
that age.—ED.

ments, and how soon he learned to carry them out to their fullest results.

Concerning our articles, those signed by John Clarke, I have to say that we do not possess such. Whatever was the original platform of the church, it is most unfortunately, with other valuable papers, we fear, irretrievably lost. The truth is, that such was the early condition of the church, it was next to impossible its records could be preserved. Dr. John Clarke himself had his own duties as a physician to attend to, the chief burden of the State evidently devolved more upon him than on any one else. The institutions of Rhode Island were principally framed and molded by him : It is generally supposed he was the author of its original code of laws. In 1651 he was sent to England to attend to the affairs of the colony, and remained there till 1664; when he returned he had, besides his church and the business of the State, his own affairs to retrieve, which had suffered much while he was engaged for the Commonwealth ; and, to crown all, there is reason to believe that his executors were unfaithful to their trusts, and that his papers under their charge were allowed to be scattered and destroyed. Those, too, who had the care of the church during the absence of Clark, and after his death, instead of recording every thing regularly in a book, placed the doings of the church on loose papers, so that by the year 1725, it was difficult to collect any of the earlier acts of the church. Only a page, as it were, here and there has been preserved, causing us to regret what is lost.

Besides a few scraps gathered up from other sources,

we have what Clarke himself considered the essence of the Baptist faith, being the propositions he proposed to defend before the ministers and magistrates of Massachusetts, while he was lying in Boston in prison, but which they declined to meet.

You may feel some interest to see them, as they show what were the sentiments insisted upon chiefly by the first pastor of an American Baptist Church, and what were the sentiments most deeply wrought into the minds of the earliest American Baptists. These propositions he has illustrated in a most satisfactory manner, showing that he was a scribe well instructed in the kingdom of heaven, and that he fed the church with the manna of the gospel. The antique, and at times, quaint mode of expression will not derogate from their value.

"The testimony of *John Clarke*, a prisoner of Jesus Christ, at *Boston*, in the behalf of my Lord, and of his people, is as followeth:

"*First* — I testify that Jesus of *Nazareth*, whom God hath raised from the dead, is made both *Lord* and Christ. This Jesus I say is the *Christ*, in English, the *Anointed* One, [and] hath a name above every name. He is the *Anointed Priest;* none to, or with Him in point of atonement. The *Anointed Prophet;* none to Him in point of instruction; the *Anointed King*, who is gone to His Father for His glorious kingdom, and shall ere long return again; and that this Jesus Christ is also *The Lord;* none to or with Him by way of commanding and ordering (with respect to the worship of God) the household of faith, which being purchased with His blood as Priest, instructed and nourished by His Spirit as Prophet, do wait in His appointment as He is the Lord, in hope of that glorious kingdom which shall ere long appear.

"*Second*—I testify that Baptism, or dipping into water, is one of the commandments of this Lord Jesus Christ, and that a visible believer, or disciple of Christ (that is, one that manifesteth repentance towards God, and faith in Jesus Christ), is the only person that is to be baptized or dipped with that visible baptism, or dipping of Jesus Christ in water; and also that visible person that is to walk in the visible order of His house; and so to wait for His coming the second time in the form of a *Lord* and *King*, with His glorious kingdom according to promise; and for His sending down (in time of His absence) the Holy Ghost, or Holy Spirit of Promise; and all this according to the last will and testament of that living Lord, whose will is not to be added to or taken from.

"*Third*—I testify, or witness, that every such believer in Christ Jesus, that waiteth for His appearing, may in point of liberty, yea, ought in point of duty, to improve that talent his Lord hath given unto him, and in the congregation may either ask for information to himself, or, if he can, may speak by way of prophecy for the edification, exhortation, and comfort of the whole; and out of the congregation at all times, upon all occasions, and in all places as far as the jurisdiction of his Lord extends, may, yea, ought to walk as a child of light, justifying wisdom with his ways, and reproving folly with the unfruitful works thereof, provided all this be shown out of a good conversation, as James speaks, with meekness of wisdom.

"*Fourth*—I testify that no such believer or servant of Jesus Christ hath any liberty, much less authority, from his Lord, to smite his fellow-servant, nor yet with outward force, or arm of flesh, to constrain or restrain his conscience, nor yet his outward man for conscience's sake, or worship of his God, where injury is not offered

to the person, name, or estate of others; every man
being such as he shall appear before the judgment seat
of Christ, and must give account of himself to God;
and therefore ought to be fully persuaded in his own
mind for what he undertakes, because he that doubteth is damned if he eat, and so also if he act, because
he doth not eat or act in faith; and what is not of faith
is sin.

" These sentiments, the supreme Lordship of Christ;
the obligation of all believers to be immersed in His
name, none but believers having any right to be baptized; the privilege of believers to improve their talents
in or out of the church; and perfect liberty of conscience to every being, were the leading truths on which
the early Baptists of this country mostly insisted, and
which constituted their joy and strength; and also
laid the foundation for that great success we witness at
this day. May we never lose sight of these foundation
principles of the Baptist cause! But to us it must seem
strange that the ministers of Massachusetts were so
afraid of these very propositions that they dared not
meet a single Baptist, and he in prison, in their defence.

"Forgive this long epistle, and receive the fraternal
regards of yours, "S. ADLAM."

CONCLUSIONS FROM THE FOREGOING.

BY THE EDITOR.

The reader will admit that what has been submitted
are *facts* and *dates,* and not opinions and theories. These
must be received until by *facts* and *dates more authentic*
these are set aside. The historical papers containing
these has been before the public and the Providence
church for seven years, and a refutation of them solic-

ited, and yet such a refutation has not been attempted. We therefore feel forced to the following conclusions:

I.

That Roger Williams neither founded nor was pastor of the present First Baptist Church in Providence, R. I.

That Roger Williams, after remaining with the society of informally baptized persons he had collected a short time only, withdrew from it as not entitled to be considered a Scriptural church; and it is more than probable that his withdrawal and opposition to the movement resulted in its *immediate dissolution.*

II.

Cotton Mather, who lived contemporaneous with Roger Williams, and wrote an Ecclesiastical History of New England, expressly declares that upon Williams' withdrawing from the society he had formed, *i. e.*, upon his turning *Seeker* and *Familist*, THE CHURCH CAME TO NOTHING.

This testimony is important, and certainly will not be questioned by Pedobaptists, to meet whose charges (that American Baptists all sprang from Roger Williams, and their baptisms from his informal baptism) we write this, because Mather was himself the most eminent Pedobaptist, and most violent hater and persecutor of Baptists of his day. Mather had the means of knowing whether that "thing like a *church*," as he called it, continued or not; and it can not be assumed that he would have written and published to the world, in almost the next town (Boston) and in the

face of the church, that it was dissolved upon Williams'
leaving it, if the church was then in existence, to deny
the charge! Can the fact be found anywhere that
any member of Williams' society, or any Baptist living
in the days of Mather, ever denied this statement?
Such a denial never was heard of, that I can learn.

But had Williams' "thing like a *church*" continued
and flourished, and been the parent of other churches,
Mather would have seized upon the fact to have prej-
udiced the world the more against the Baptists, pointing to the invalidity of their baptisms and ordinances,
owing to their informal origin, as Pedobaptists now
endeavor to do. But this Mather did not do, because
he could not; for he affirms that the "thing" soon
came to nothing—and long before he wrote this there
was no such "thing" in existence. Williams gathered
the "thing" in March, and repudiated and left it in July
following. It was only a "thing" of a day. If then,
the last remains of the only thing called a Baptist
Church, with which Williams had any connection or
anything to do, vanished from the earth so soon, having
in the days of Mather no successor, the reader must
conclude that Williams' society was not the prolific
mother of the Baptist Churches of New England, much
less of America, for it never had a church child—it was
itself an abortion.

III.

My third conclusion is, that the present First Church
in Providence was not founded by Roger Williams,
nor was he ever the pastor of it a day, or an hour, nor
12

of any Baptist Church in existence; since, as has been proved above, the only "*thing*" like a church with which he had any connection, had but an experimental existence, *without having originated another church* or *leaving a successor.*

IV.

I am forced to conclude from the dates submitted, that the First Church in Providence was first organized in 1652, and did not hold at first the faith now held by Baptists, but was a schism or succession from a regular Baptist Church that had existed in Providence some years before it.

V.

I can see how the First Church in Providence came to have its present confused history and false dates. It had no records or written history for the first century of its existence; and its present records were compiled principally from *oral* history, inferences, and suppositions. The church from which the present Providence First Church came, had died out, and it was supposed that the present church was the legitimate offspring and successor of that church, which is not the fact, for it was a schism : and it was supposed that that perverted church was the successor or offspring of Williams' society—which was not the fact; and knowing well that Williams gathered his society in March, 1639, the compiler of the records of the Providence church dated the origin of the present church with the baptism of Roger Williams—*i. e.*, gave it the date of Williams' society — perhaps, not unwilling for the Providence church to enjoy the *prestige* of being the oldest Baptist Church in America, and the *eclat* of so illustrious a founder as Roger Williams.

VI.

It can also be seen from the *dates* submitted, that, without contesting the age of the Providence church, granting her the year 1639 as the year of her birth, and that she is the veritable successor of that "*thing like a church*," which Williams gathered, still she is not the oldest Baptist Church in America, by at least one full year.

For the facts and dates submitted show that Dr. John Clarke came to Newport in the year 1638, and soon after his arrival organized a Baptist Church, and the evidence is satisfactory that, though scattered for a season, while the British held possession of the island, it has never ceased to exist, and that the present First Baptist Church in Newport is its successor and representative. That 1638, and not 1644, is the true date of the founding of the Newport church, is established beyond controversy by a fact stated in a note at the bottom of the 455th page of Minutes of the Philadelphia Association, published by the American Publication Society. (*See the note to which I called Mr. Adlam's attention, and his remarks.*) From this note, and it is as authentic as conclusive, that in 1738 the church of Newport was one hundred years old, and it was therefore founded in 1638. That upon that occasion John Callender, its then pastor, preached a sermon upon the occasion. I consider this note of itself as putting a

full end to the controversy about the age of the Newport church—as Mather's statement does to the claim
that Rogers Williams founded the present First Church
in Providence.

VII.

I conclude that the First Baptist Church in Newport is older by one year, even should we allow the date
claimed by the Providence church to be the true date;
while if 1652 is its true date, and the Newport church
was founded (as is claimed by some without proof) in
1644; when all admit she was in existence, then is the
Newport church eight years older than the Providence
church.

But if 1652 is the true birth-year of the Providence
church, as has been shown, and 1638 the true birth-
year of the Newport church, as has been shown—then
is the Newport church fourteen years older than her
rival.

VIII.

There is a conclusion bearing upon the use Pedobaptists make of the claims of the Providence church,
which may be stated here. That but *very few* Baptist
Churches in America or New England have any ecclesiastical connection with either the church in Newport
or Providence. Baptists ministers coming over from
England and Wales, as well as from the Continent,
raised up churches in different parts of the country,
from New England to South Carolina, and these have
since multiplied all over the land. It is said truly by

an author who has recently examined the period we
we have been discussing, and he freely conceded the
priority claimed by the Newport church:

"They are connected in part with the Baptists of
England, whose origin, in their turn, is derived from
the Baptists of the European Continent, (reaching back
to apostolic days), and from the Baptists, who from
the early ages of the church were nurtured in Wales;
and they are directly connected in part with the Cam-
bro-British Baptists, who have preserved in the moun-
tain fastnesses of their native land, (Wales), the principles and practices which they received from their
fathers, and from their fathers' fathers, from the ancient
times of Christianity. Thus the chain which unites
them to the early Baptist Churches, is a chain of triple
link, which can not easily be broken."

IX

There is a final conclusion due to a man, Dr. John
Clarke, as well as to the Baptist denomination. One
of the wrongs resulting from the false date of the Providence church is the undue prominence given to Roger
Williams as a Baptist, while the life, and prominent
labors, and sacrifices of Dr. John Clarke and Holmes,
are scarcely known.

It is greatly to be regretted that any one was ever so
mislead as to proclaim to the world that Roger Williams was the first man to conceive and advocate the
idea of religous liberty, and that he was the father and
founder of the American Baptist Churches. Both of
these statements are utterly false. The Baptists of every
age have been the sole advocates of religous liberty in

its fullest sense.* They advocated it in opposition to Papist and Protestants in England, in the pulpit, by their pens, and by martyrdom. Williams confessedly borrowed his views of soul liberty from them. He was indebted to Baptists and not the Baptists to him. He has no claim to be acknowledged a Baptist, and better would it be for his memory if his short and abortive religious Baptistical life was obliterated from the pages of history, and the memory of men. For a man, only four months associated with a handful of informally baptized men and then renouncing his baptism and all existing church organizations and ordinances as illegal and void, to be lauded and eulogized as the father and founder of American Baptists, is silly and absurd.

As a bold and poweful advocate of civil and religious liberty, and for all he did in conjunction with Clarke in framing and securing the Charter of Rhode Island, I do him homage; but as a Baptist we owe him nothing. As a religionist he had the courage to suffer, but he was uninstructed, unstable, and visionary.

There is another name, long, too long concealed by Williams being placed before him, who will after times be regarded with unmingled affection and respect, as the true pioneer of the Baptist cause in the New World. "That orb of purest lustre will yet shine forth, and Baptists, whether they regard his spotless character, his talents, his learning, the services he rendered, the ur-

---

* See Orchard's History of Foreign Baptists, Vol. I; English Baptists, Vol. II. Every Baptist should procure and read these; and every man who wishes a correct knowledge of church history.

banity and modesty that distinguished him, will mention John Clarke as the real founder of the First Church
upon the American soil."

Again I say—all honor to Williams, and gratitude
be his for what, as a *man*, but not as a *Baptist*, he did.
He indeed reached forward and grasped at the Baptist
standard, but his heart faltered, his eye dimmed, his
hand trembled and fell. That banner was reared and
sustained in defiance of prisons and stripes unto blood,
by hands in Newport, and its conquests carried into
the very heart of Massachusetts, and a work was commenced by John Clarke and his suffering coadjutors,
which will continue to spread and triumph

> Till the waves of the bay where the Mayflower lay,
> Shall foam and freeze no more!

NOTE.—PROF. CLARKE has so fully covered the ground of
Dr. Adlam's Historical Address that I find it quite needless to
publish it.

AN AUTHENTIC HISTORY

OF THE

FIRST BAPTIST CHURCH OF NEWPORT, R. I.

AND OF THE

FIRST CHURCH OF AMERICA.

THE history of the First Baptist Church of Newport dates from the earliest settlement on this island. In March, 1638, a colony from Boston, driven by intolerance and persecution, emigrated southward into the unbroken wilderness. After a painful and perilous journey they came at last to a place called by the Indians Aquidneck; or, the Isle of Peace. Here they made their first settlement, near the north end of the island, in what is now the town of Portsmouth. The leading spirit of this enterprise was John Clarke, an English scholar and *preacher*, who arrived in Massachusetts in November, 1637. Soon after the colony was established a church was formed, of which Mr. Clarke became the pastor. There is little reason to doubt that this was a Baptist Church, for it was composed largely, if not wholly, of Baptist believers, and was presided over by a minister whose doctrinal views are known to have been closely akin to the cardinal tenets of our denomination.

In April, 1639, several families, including all the officers of government, who carried with them their official records, removed to the southern part of the island and founded the city of Newport. It is believed, on good authority, that the church organization formed at Portsmouth was carried to the new settlement at the same time. At least there was very soon a Baptist Church in Newport comprising many of the same members and under the care of the same pastor, Dr. John Clarke. This remarkable man, who was at once the pastor of the church, the head of the government, and the resident physician, was born·in 1609, and educated at one of the English ·universities. At the age 26 he came to America, but his religious opinions became obnoxious to the authorities at Boston, and he was exposed to public opprobrium on that account. Finding that liberty of conscience was denied him in Massachusetts, he planned and executed the bold project of planting a new State on the shores of Narragansett Bay. And until death his guiding hand may be traced in all the affairs of the infant commonwealth. Most wisely did he administer the business of the colony and the church. With rare devotion and self-sacrifice he addressed himself to the task or organizing and developing the new province. With unswerving consistency did he contend for the faith once delivered to the saints. There was much contention in the colony over civil and religious questions. Divers opinions abounded which gendered much strife. But in each dispute Mr. Clarke displayed excellent tact and judgment, taking almost invariably the position which in the end proved right and safe.

In 1650, a controversy arose which involved several fundamental questions; the extent and limitations of religious liberty; the authority of the Word of God, and the gospel warrant for church organizations. With Robert Lenthall and others, Mr. Clarke took very decided ground maintaining (1) the scriptural authority for a visible church with public ordinances against those who would spiritualize them away, (2) the supremacy of the Word of God in the province of morals and religion against those who would supersede it by an inward illumination, (3) the restriction of the exercise of freedom within the limits prescribed by the Holy Scriptures against those who confused liberty with license. As a result of these debates the church was divided. A part following an inner light became "Seekers" and afterward "Quakers."

The doctrine of the imposition of hands upon all believers began to be seriously discussed as early as 1656. Four years later a six-principle church was organized by seceding members from the First Church. There was agitation also over the question of the Sabbath, and a few persons who favored the observance of Saturday withdrew (1671) and formed a Sabbatarian church.

Mr. Clarke went to England in the interests of the colony in 1651, where he remained till he had secured

the great charter of 1663.* He then returned and
resumed his duties which were not laid down till his
death, which occurred April 20, 1676.

Obadiah Holmes, the second pastor, was born in
Preston, Lancashire, England, about 1606, and educated at the University of Oxford. He came to this
country in 1639, and united with the Congregational
Church in Salem, Mass. Six years later he removed to
Rehoboth, where, with several others whose religious
connections were changed, he was baptized (1649) by
Mr. Clarke, and at once formed a Baptist Church in
that place. After a precarious existence of two years
this organization was broken up by the Plymouth magistrates, whereupon Mr. Holmes with many others came
to Newport. He seems to have been associated with
Mr. Clarke in the pastoral office, and after the latter's
death assumed full charge of the church. Sent by the
church as a messenger to Lynn in 1651, he was seized
by the magistrates and severely whipped for his bold
avowal of Baptist principles. Mark Lucar and Joseph
Torrey were elders in the church at this time. The
latter also held several offices in the colony, and was
ssociated with Mr. Holmes in charge of the church
during Mr. Clarke's absence in England.

The first deacon was William Weeden who died in
1676. The second was Philip Smith who was living in
1692. It may be further noted that Robert Lenthall
who had attempted in 1638 to form a Baptist Church
in Weymouth, became two years later a freeman at

---

* The reader will see that Roger Williams had no hand in securing this
Charter, which secured full and free religious liberty to all.

Newport where he taught the first public school in America, if not in the world; that Thomas Painter had been publicly whipped in Hingham for refusing to bring his child to the baptismal font; that John Cooke, once a Congregationalist minister, was, in 1694, the oldest surviving male passenger of the Mayflower; that Philip Edes had been a friend and helper of Oliver Cromwell; that Samuel Hubbard after long struggles found the light of truth, and at his death left many valuable manuscripts, which have been of incalculable service to subsequent historians. Singing in public worship was from the first approved and practiced. Mr. Holmes died October 15, 1681. For some five years the church had no pastor. Probably its affairs were administered by the elders of whom mention has been made.

The third pastor was Richard Dingley. Little is known of him or his labors here. He came to America and was received into the Baptist Church some time in 1684. Four years afterward he was ordained as pastor of this church. This relation continued five years, but no important details of the church life during this period have come down to us. Mr. Dingley resigned and removed to South Carolina in 1694.

After his departure there was an interregnum of seventeen years in which the church, though without the watchcare of a regular pastor, seems to have enjoyed a good degree of prosperity. In November, 1711, William Peckham was ordained and settled over the church, and continued in that office till his death in 1732.

John Comer, the fifth pastor, was born in Boston,

August 1, 1704, educated at Yale College, baptized at Boston, January 31, 1725, and ordained at Newport as colleague with Mr. Peckham, May 19, 1726. His strenuous advocacy of the doctrine of the imposition of hands led in 1729 to a rupture of the pastoral relation. Mr. Comer died at Rehoboth, Mass., at the early age of thirty years.

The old meeting-house in "Green End" in which the church had worshiped, was sold in 1707, and Singing, which had fallen into disuse, was reintroduced. new edifice built on Tanner street the year following.

A church covenant was adopted in 1727. Several names should be mentioned: Daniel White " an assistant to the pastor," James Barker, "an elder," Peter Taylor, Samuel Maxwell and Wm. Peckham, deacons, Peter Foulger, the maternal grandfather of Benjamin Franklin, Thomas Dungan, the first Baptist minister in Pennsylvania, also the three sons of the second pastor, Obadiah, John and Jonathan Holmes.

John Callender, a native of Boston, and graduate of Harvard, became pastor of the church October 13, 1731. On the 24th of March, 1738, the pastor preached an historical discourse reviewing the events of the century. During the same year a new meeting-house was built on the present site. Mr. Callender's pastoral relations were terminated by his death, which occurred January 26, 1745.

Before the close of the year Edward Upham was called to the pastorate. He was born in Malden, Mass., in 1709; graduated at Harvard in 1734. During his administration the first Baptist college in the country was founded—the same institution that finally located at Providence and became Brown University. Mr. Upham resigned in 1771.

The next pastor, Erasmus Kelley, was born and educaled in Pennsylvania. His period of service (1771 to 1784) covered the stormy times of the Revolutionary War. In 1778, the British troops took possession· of the meeting-house, and the church was scattered. The war fell with terrible effect on Newport, completely paralyzing its industries. Mr. Kelley, with many others, fled from the town at the approach of the British army, but came back on the conclusion of peace, in 1787, and gathered the church again. Death terminated his labors in November of the same year.

The pastoral office was next filled by the choice of Benjamin Foster who began his labors with the church on the first Lord's day in January, 1785. He was born in Danvers, Mass., June 12, 1750; graduated at Yale in 1714, and baptized by the Rev. Samuel Stillman, with whom he also studied theology. In September of 1788, he resigned and removed to New York, where he died ten years latter. Under his leadership the church joined the Warren Association. Dr. Watts' Psalms and Hymns superseded Tate and Brady's collection. Among the prominent names of this epoch, were Samuel Fowler, a member of the last Colonial Assembly of Rhode Island, which passed the act severing the colony from Great Britian; William Claggett, celebrated for his clocks and for anticipating Franklin in some of his experiments with electricity; Hezekiah Carpenter and Josiah Lyndon, both generous benefactors of the church; Benjamin Hall and Joseph Pike made deacons in 1785.

Reviewing the history of the church, thus far traversed, we find a noble record. Strong men, of wide reaching influence and broad plans, were connected with the church. Its ministry was able and cultivated. With scarcely an exception, the pastors were men of University training. Benedict having brought his account of the church down to 1788, adds this remark: "We have now followed the successors of pastors of this ancient community for about a century and a half, and what is singular in our denomination in early times of these nine pastors, all but Mr. Peckham were men of liberal education."

In all its long and honorable history, the First Baptist Church in Newport has contended earnestly for the faith once delivered to the saints, and held unswervingly to the cardinal principles of our Christian doctrine. As in past generations, so in those to come, it will maintain its unyielding allegiance to the truth as it is in Jesus.

Its Pastors—Term of Service.

NAMES.	BEGAN.	CLOSED.
John Clarke,	1638	1676
Obadiah Holmes,	1681	1682
Richard Dingley,	1689	1694
William Peckham,	1711	1732
John Comer,	1726	1729
John Callender,	1731	1748
Edward Upham,	1749	1771
Erasmus Kelley,	1771	1784

Its Pastors—Term of Service—*Continued.*

NAMES.	BEGAN.	CLOSED.
Benjamin Foster,	1758	1788
Michael Eddy,	1789	1835
Arthur A. Ross,	1835	1848
Joseph Smith,	1841	1849
Samuel Adlam,	1849	1864
Comfort E. Barrows,	1865	1883
Francio W. Ryder,	1884	

NOTE.—The First Church at Providence can show no such a record as this. It never had any, and knows not who founded it, or who were its pastors.

Its Covenant—Adopted May 4, 1727.

We, who desire to walk together in the fear of the Lord, do, by the help and influence of the Holy Ghost, profess our deep sense of sin and humiliation therefor.

And in the presence of the great God, the elect angels, and one another, having a sense of our unworthiness considered of ourselves, and looking wholly and alone to the Lord Jesus Christ for worthiness and acceptance, we do now solemnly give up ourselves to the Lord in a church state, according to the prime constitution of the gospel church; that He may be our God, and we His people, through the everlasting covenant of His free grace.

Submitting to Jesus Christ as the King and Head of His Church, embracing Him as the Prophet, Priest and King of our salvation, and desiring to conform to all His holy laws and ordinances for our growth, establishment and consolation, that we may be a holy spouse unto Him; being fully satisfied in the way of church communion, and of the truth of grace on each other's soul in some good measure, we do now solemnly, in the name and fear of God, join ourselves together in a holy union and fellowship, humbly submitting to the discipline of the gospel, and all holy duties, which our spiritual relation enjoins and requires.

And, by the help of divine grace, without which we can do nothing, we promise to walk in all godliness, humility, and brotherly love, so that our communion may be delightful to God, and comfortable to ourselves and the rest of the Lord's people.

We promise to watch over each other's conversation, and not to suffer sin upon one another as God shall discover it to us, or any of us; to stir up each other to love and good works, and, if any fall into sin, to warn and admonish them according to the nature of the the offense, with a spirit of meekness, as the gospel requires.

We promise, and engage to pray with, and for one another, as God shall enable us from time to time, for the glory of this church, that the presence of God may be in it, and His spirit rest upon it, and His protection be over it, that it may be increased with the increase of God.

We promise to bear one another's burdens, weaknesses, short-comings, and infirmities, and not to acquaint any without the garden of Christ of them, but to observe the rule of Christ in such cases.

We promise to strive together for the truth of the gospel, and the purity of God's ordinances; and to endeavor to pass a Christian construction upon those who, in some lesser and extra fundamental points,
13

differ from us. We will endeavor to keep the unity
of the spirit, in the bond of peace, with all that hold
the head, Jesus Christ, both their Lord and ours. We
promise not to retain a Pharisaical spirit to withdraw
in time of prayer, but to join with all such as, in the
ground of charity, are true believers and churches of
Christ.

We promise to observe the public worship of God on
Lord's days, and at other times, as God may afford
opportunity, and strive, what in us lies, for each other's
edification.

Each and every one of these things we humbly submit to in the name and fear of God, promising, and
purposing to perform, not in our own strength, being
conscious of our own weakness, but in the power and
strength of the blessed God, whose redeemed ones we
trust we are, and whom we sincerely desire to serve.
To whom be glory in all the churches, now and evermore.   Amen.

Its Articles of Faith.

[These will be interesting to all Baptists, and perhaps many of
our churches and brethren about to organize would like to adopt
them, and so hold the faith of the First Baptist Church organized
on this continent. All can see there is not a scintilla of Calvinism in them. Baptists were sound, held and taught in *all* the faith
once delivered to the saints, fifteen hundred years before Calvin
was born. What *he added to it* is Calvinism, and that we most
heartily repudiate.—EDITOR.]

I.

WE believe that the Holy Bible was written by men
divinely inspired;   that it is the only rule of Christian

faith and practice,[2] and that it teaches the following doctrines:

1 1 Tim. iii. 16. 2 Pet. i. 19–21. Rom. ii. 12. Luke xxiv. 44–46. John x. 34–35. Matt. v. 17–18. John v. 36–39, 45–47. John xiv. 26. John xvi. 12–15. Gal. i. 6–12, 2 Pet. iii. 15–16.

2 2 Tim. iii. 15–17. 2 Pet. i. 19–21. Matt. v. 19. John xii. 47–48. Matt. i. 5–9.

II.

There is one God,[1] self-existent,[2] infinite in every natural and moral excellence.[3] He has revealed himself as existing in three persons: the Father, the Son (or the Word), and the Holy Spirit.[4] These three are one in respect to divine essence, though differing in the relations they bear to one another and to created beings.[5]

1 Deut. vi. 4. Isa. xlv. 21–22.

2 Ex. iii. 13–15. Isa. xlii. 10.

3 Deut. xxxii. 4. Ex. xxxiv. 6–7. Ps. xxxvi. 5–9. Matt. v. 48. 1 Pet. i. 14–17.

4 Matt. xxviii, 19. Matt. iii, 16–17. 2 Cor. xiii. 14. 1 Cor. xii. 3–6. John i. 1–13. John xiv. 26. John xv. 26. John xvi. 13–14. Acts v. 3–4. Acts v. 3–4. 1 Cor. iii. 16–17.

5 John i. 1–2. John v. 17–30. John xvi. 14–15. John xvii. 5–24. Heb. i. 1–4. Col. i. 15–17. Rev. xxi. 22–23.

III.

Man was created holy,[1] but by willful disobedience to God he fell from that state of holiness and became guilty and depraved.[2] In consequence of this fall the whole human race is depraved.[3] Moreover all responsible human beings have actually sinned and are justly exposed to condemnation in the sight of God.[4] The sinful character of men consists in this, that they are destitute of love to God and self-willed, instead of obedient to him.[5]

1 Gen. i. 27-31. Rom. v. 12.
2 Gen. iii. 1-7. Rom. v. 12-19.
3 Rom. v. 19-21. John iii. 6-7. Eph. ii. 1-3.
4 Rom. iv. 9-12, 19, 20, 23. Gal. ii. 16. Gal. iii. 10-22.
5 Matt. xxii. 25-40. Rom. xiii. 8-10. John iii. 4. Ps. xxxvi. 1. Rom. 1. 31-38. Jer. ii. 13. Jer. xvii. 9-10. Rom. viii. 7. Eph. ii. 3. John v. 40.

IV.

The only way of deliverance from this state of sin and condemnation is through the sacrifice of Jesus Christ[1] who is the Eternal Word in personal union with human nature.[2] He freely offered himself as a substitute to suffer and **die in behalf of all men.**[3] Thus he became a perfect savior[4] **by whom all who will may be saved.**[5] All men are invited to accept Him as the savior of their souls,[6] and *to all who do so accept Him He is the actual ground of justification and eternal life.*[7]

1 Luke xix. 10. John iii. 36. 1 John v. 12. Acts iv. 12.
2 John i. 1-5. John ix. 14. Rom. ix. 5. 1 Tim. ii. 5.
3 2 Cor. v. 14, 15, 21. 1 Pet. v. 24. Matt. xx. 28. Heb. ix. 13-14. Heb. ii. 9.
4 Rom. iii. 20-26. Heb. ix. 26. Heb. x. 10-18. Heb. vii. 25. John i. 29.
5 Acts xvi. 30-31. Acts xii. 38-39. John vi. 37. 1 Tim. ii. 4. 2 Pet. iii. 9. Rev. xxii. 17.
6 John vi. 29-35. John vii. 37. 1 John iii. 23. Matt. xix. 28. Isa. lv. 1-7.
7 1 Tim. iv. 10. 2 Cor. v. 17. Rom. v. 1-5. Rom. x. 4. John iii. 16, 18, 36.

V.

Those who truly obey the gospel were chosen in Christ before the foundation of the world by Him who sees the end from the beginning,[1] and in consequence of God's purpose and grace they are regenerated by the Holy Spirit,[2] without whose influence none would ever repent and believe.[3]

1 Eph. i. 3–6. 2 Thess. ii. 13. 2 Tim. i. 9. Rom. viii. 28–29. 1 Pet. i. 1–5. John i. 13.
2 2 Pet. i. 2–2. James i. 18. Eph. ii. 8–10. Titus iii. 4–7. Rom. ix. 16.
3 John iii. 3–8. Acts ii. 33. Acts v. 31. 2 Tim. ii. 25. Gal. v. 22–23. 1 John ii. 29. 1 John iv. 7. 2 John v. 1–4.

VI.

Nothing can separate true believers from the love of God,[1] but they will be kept by the power of God through faith unto salvation.[2] The sure and final proof that they are true believers consists in the continuance of their attachment and obedience to Christ until the end of life.[3]

1 John x. 27–29. John vi. 39–40. John v. 24. Rom. viii. 31–39.
2 1 Pet. i. 3–5. Philip i. 6. 1 Thess. v. 23–24.
3 Col. i. 21–23. Heb. iii. 14. 1 Cor. ix. 26–27. 2 Pet. i. 10. Philip ii. 12–13.

VII.

A church is a company of believers organized for the observance of the ordinances and the promotion of Christ's kingdom.[1] Each church is independent and self-governed though in fraternal fellowship with other churches.[2] The officers of a church are pastors and deacons.[3]

1 Acts xxix. 41–47. Acts ix. 22–26. Acts xv. 3, 4. 41. Gal. i. 2. 1 Cor. i. 2, 13–14. 1 Cor. vi. 11. 1 Cor. xi. 18–22. 1 Cor. xiv.
2 1 Cor. v. 4–5, 13. 2 Cor. ii. 5–8. Matt. xviii. 15–17. 1 Cor. xvi. 1. Acts xv.
3 Acts xx. 17–28. Philip i. 1. 1 Tim. iii. 1–13. Titus i. 5–9. 1 Pet. v. 1–4.

VIII.

The ordinances of the church are Baptism and the Lord's Supper.[1] Baptism is the first formal act of the Christian life.[2] It is immersion in water, into the name of the Father, and of the Son and of the Holy Spirit,[3] and is administered only to professed believers in Christ.[4] The Lord's Supper is observed in commemoration of the death of Christ, [5] and follows baptism.[6]

1 Matt. xviii. 19–20. 1 Cor. ix. 23–26.

2 Acts ii. 37–41. Acts xxii. 16. Acts xviii. 8. Acts xvi. 14. Acts xv. 32–34. John iii. 5. Gal. ii. 26–27.

3 Matt. iii. 16. Acts viii. 38–39. Rom. vi. 34. Col. ii. 12.

4 1 Pet. iii. 21. Mark i. 4. Rom. vi. 1–6. Gal. iii. 26–27. Eph. iv. 5.

5 Matt. xxvi. 26–30. 1 Cor. xi. 23–26.

6 1 Cor. xi. 18–22.

IX.

The first day of the week is to be observed as the Lord's Day, in commemoration of the resurrection of Christ from the dead.[1]

1 John xx. 19–26. 1 Cor. xvi. 1–2. Acts xx. 7. Rev. i. 10. Compare Gen. ii. 2–3 and Ex. xx. 8–11.

X.

There will be a resurrection of the dead[1] and a final judgment[2] at the time of Christ's second coming.[3] Then the wicked will go away into everlasting punishment[4] but the righteous into life eternal.[5] *

1 John v. 28–29. 1 Cor. xi.

2 2 Col. v. 5, 10. Matt. xxv. 31, 46.

3 Acts i. 11 2 Tim. iv. 1.

4 2 Thess. i. 6–10. Mark ix. 43–48. Matt. v. 26.

5 John xiv. 2–3. 1 John iii. 2. Rev. iii. 12. Rev. xx.

* This is the only statement to which exception can be taken. The righteous dead alone will be raised at the second coming of Christ, to be rewarded according to their works; and the wicked dead only to be judged at the final judgment according to their works. See Rev. xx. It will also be seen that the Lord's Supper was held as a Church Ordinance, and Church Ordinances can not be carried out of the church.—EDITOR.

Part Third

A BRIEF HISTORICAL STATEMENT

CONCERNING MY VISIT TO THE

FIRST BAPTIST CHURCH IN

AMERICA FOUNDED BY

JOHN CLARKE

IN 1638

Also my two visits to the church in Providence

CONRAD N. GLOVER

Th.B., D.D., D.B., D.C.H.

1966

This chapter has been written upon the request of Dr. O. H. Griffith, Editor-in-Chief of the American Baptist Association Publications.

PREFACE

The writer was delighted when he learned there was to be a reprint of **The First Baptist Church in America** by Dr. J. R. Graves and Dr. S. Adlam. He was very pleased to learn that Dr. C. N. Glover was to write a section to be added to the book, and he was flattered when Dr. Glover asked him to write a preface to this addition.

Conrad Nathan Glover is the son of the late Rev. Robert W. Glover and Mary Young Glover. His early parental discipline, his early education and training in the Philadelphia and Harmony Missionary Baptist churches, and his experiences in life, started him in the right direction. When the Lord saved him and then called him to preach, he was by environment and circumstance placed in the first classes of the Missionary Baptist College, Sheridan, Arkansas. He was a rural mail carrier but he had time to devote to his studies and finished about every course the college offered.

Dr. Glover has few peers as an educator, scholar, theologian, preacher and speaker. His keen sense of right and wrong, his lifetime training, discipline, associates and environment, eminently fit him for this assignment.

The simple and straightforward manner of his approach to truth, his diligent search for it and his joy at being able to give this truth to others, make reading after him a joy. The reader will not only understand what Dr. Glover has written but will have a keener insight and better understanding of what Dr. Graves and Dr. Adlam have written in their sections of the book.

The writer knows some of the conclusions reached in this book are not popular with some men, but is it not so that most truth is not popular with the masses? But the truths revealed, if accepted by the readers and put into practice in their lives, will bring honor and glory to our Lord. They will also bring from Him, the writer believes, a welcome plaudit which will be appreciated through all eternity.

—A. T. Powers.

The First Baptist Church in America
1966

In September of 1937, I attended a National Convention of the American Legion in New York City, and from there I made a tour of New England and Canada. In planning the New England trip, I scheduled a visit to the so-called Roger Williams Church in Providence, Rhode Island. I had read the book, **The First Baptist Church in America Not Founded by Roger Williams.** This book was compiled by Graves and Adlam. I took a copy of the Graves and Adlam History with me on the trip in view of making some comparisons of what I saw and what was published in the book.

The Roger Williams Church

When I visited the Roger Williams Church, I stood by the cornerstone and opened the Graves and Adlam book to page seventeen, where they published the inscription found on a tablet placed upon the walls of its audience room. The inscription published by them is as follows:

> "This church was founded in 1639, by Roger Williams, its first pastor, and the first asserter of Liberty of Conscience. It was the first church in Rhode Island and the first Baptist church in America."
>
> (Graves Copyright is dated 1890)

What Dr. Adlam, who was pastor of the New-

205

port church, found said "1639," and what I found written upon the cornerstone said "1638." I shall never forget the feeling that came over me at that time. I wondered then, and I still am made to wonder, why the change was made. I do not want to believe that this change was deliberately made in order to lay a claim to being the oldest Baptist Church in America, but you have the Adlam quote at the top of page seventeen in his book, and I am furnishing a picture of the cornerstone to verify my statement.

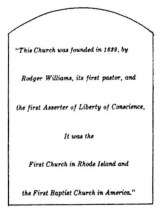

"*This Church was founded in 1639, by*

Rodger Williams, its first pastor, and

the first Asserter of Liberty of Conscience,

It was the

First Church in Rhode Island and

the First Baptist Church in America."

Inasmuch as I have a list of the names of all of the pastors of the Roger Williams Church, and the dates they served, I pass them on to the reader of this sketch.

They are in order as follows:

Roger Williams	
Chad Brown	
Thomas Olney	1638-1718
William Wickenden	
Gregory Dexter	
Pardon Tillinghast	
Erenezer Jenckes	1719-1726
James Brown	1732
Samuel Winsor	1733-1758
Thomas Burlingame	1733
Samuel Winsor, Jr.	1759-1771
James Manning	1771-1791
John Stanford	1788-1789
Jonathan Maxcy	1791-1792
Stephen Gano	1792-1828
Robert E. Pattison	1830-1836
William Hague	1837-1840
Robert E. Pattison	1840-1842
James N. Granger	1842-1857
Samuel L. Caldwell	1858-1873
Edward G. Taylor	1875-1881
Thomas Edwin Brown	1882-1890
Henry Melville King	1891-1906
Elijah Abraham Hanley	1907-1911
John F. Vichert	1912-1916
Albert B. Cohoe	1916-1920
Arthur W. Cleaves	1922-1940
Albert C. Thomas	1941-1954
Homer L. Trickett	1955-1964

after that?

Together with my wife, Gladys Glover, and our daughter, Mary Beth Glover, we visited the Roger Williams Church in 1964. On this visit, I met the pastor, Homer L. Trickett.

I have read much concerning Roger Williams, and nowhere have I seen any attempt to refute the statements in history that his baptism was spurious.

When the baptism of Roger Williams is tried by the Scriptures, and the fact that the church is the only authority to evangelize people and organize other churches, I cannot accept the fact that Roger Williams was indeed a Baptist, nor recognize the church which bears his name as being a scriptural Baptist Church.

I offer the following quotation from **A History of the Baptists in New England** by Henry S. Burrage, D.D. On pages 22 and 23 of the text of Burrage's History published in 1894 appears the following:

> "The religious opinions of Williams and his associates were evidently in a transition state. The tendency of the former had been toward Baptist views for some time. Before leaving England he had been acquainted with Baptists, and was familiar with their articles of belief; and he was doubtless the leader in the formation of a Baptist church at Providence. The first sign of organization was at some time prior to **March 16, 1639** (emphasis mine), when

Mr. Williams was baptized by Ezekiel Holliman, and he in turn baptized Holliman and 'some ten more.' But Williams remained only a few months in connection with the church. He had doubts in reference to the validity of his own baptism, and the baptism of his associates on account of the absence of 'authorized administrators.' For him there was no church and no ministry left. The apostolic succession was interrupted and apostolic authority had ceased. It was the baptizer, and not the baptism about which he doubted. He was a high church Anabaptist. He went out of the church, left his little congregation behind, preached when and where he could, and became a 'seeker' the rest of his days. And during the rest of his days he never came to a 'satisfying discovery' of a true church or ministry."

I can arrive at no other conclusion concerning Roger Williams' views concerning the continuity of the church from the days of Christ and the apostles than that he was of the opinion that at some time before his day the church had so apostatized that it ceased to exist in the world, and with its passing the authority to administer baptism was lost to the world. He found in John Clarke a companionable friend, and went so far as to say he believed the baptism practiced by John Clarke came nearer the practice of the founder of the church, Jesus Christ, than any other practice of religion; still, he was in doubt as to the authority by which it was done. The evidence is that Williams remained friendly with the Baptists as long as he lived.

Roger Williams was sound in his declarations touching on the plan of salvation. He contended that repentance toward God, and faith in the Lord Jesus Christ were prerequisites to regeneration. He believed the church must be composed of a regenerated membership.

I do not agree that the idea of soul liberty began with Roger Williams, but there is no doubt he was an advocate of it during his lifetime: it was a matter of conscience with him. He left England so that he might be free in his religion, and later was banished from Massachusetts for pressing his views on liberty of conscience and separation of church and state.

From the Baptist point of view, Roger Williams is to be highly commended for leaving a congregation, organized by him, when his conscience and his knowledge of the Scriptures caused him to know that the congregation, though called a Baptist Church, existed without scriptural baptism, and therefore, could not be a scriptural church. Such a church was not commissioned by Jesus Christ to preach the gospel or to administer the ordinances.

History reveals the fact that Roger Williams was truly a great man. I would not in the least take from him his rightful place among the great men of his time, or any other time. I believe him to have been a Baptist at heart, and the record speaks for itself with reference to his being the first strong advocate for the separation of church and state in the American Colonies. I accept the record as teaching that he did the best he could with the light he had. He would accept nothing by compromise, and died with a longing in his heart for the peace that only the right relationship with Christ and His church brings to a human soul.

Yes, I stood in the Roger Williams Church in Providence, Rhode Island, in 1937, and I again stood in the church in 1964. (I was photographed standing in the high pulpit.) I stood there moved by mingled emotions. A thing venerable with age, the building and furnishings superlative in design and workmanship, a thing of beauty that holds you spellbound, and yet, the history of its beginning is ever present in the mind to keep you from enjoying the closeness of spiritual fellowship that otherwise any Baptist should have while there.

Roger Williams died in 1683 and was buried in solemnity by those who loved him.

(I have some pictures of the interior of the church, but before I was granted permission to take the pictures, I had to sign an agreement that the pictures would not be used for publication.)

The Roger Williams Church

I was so impressed by the church house, or as it is referred to in their publications, "The Meeting House," that doubtless some statements about the building would be of interest and information to the reader.

The following is a quote from a brief historical statement which I obtained at the church house:

> "For sixty years this church had no house of worship and held its services in the homes of the members or under the trees. Its first house of worship was built in 1700 by Rev. Pardon Tillinghast, the sixth pastor, and deeded to the church in 1711. It stood at the corner of Main Street and Smith Street. This gave place to a larger one, built on the same spot in 1726, which was forty feet square."

The present church house is located on a one and one-fourth acre tract of land about one-eighth of a mile south of where the other two buildings stood. It was begun in 1774 and dedicated in May, 1775. Rhode Island College was constituted in the Annual Session of the Messenger Assembly of the Philadelphia Association in 1764. I quote from the minutes of that year:

> "Agreed, to inform the churches to which we respectively belong, that, inasmuch as a charter is obtained in Rhode Island government, toward erecting a Baptist college, the churches should be liberal in contributing toward carrying the same into execution."

This college was located in Warren, Rhode Island, and remained there until 1771 when it was moved to Providence, Rhode Island. The purpose as set forth for the building of the church house in Providence was as follows: "For the Public Worship of Almighty God; and also for holding Commencement in." The name of the college was changed from Rhode Island College, to Brown University in 1804. The original plan was to build a church house sixty feet square, which was to cost "5,000 pounds sterling," but when it was decided to hold the university commencement exercises in the building it was decided to build it eighty feet square at a cost of "7,000 pounds sterling." As to how the additional money was raised to erect the building, I quote from an **Historical Statement** by Rev. Henry M. King, D.D.:

> "This additional sum was raised, as was the common method in the case of large undertakings of that time—but the first and only instance in the history of this church—by an officially authorized lottery."

The seating capacity of the church house is 800 on the main floor and 600 in the gallery. It is still the largest non-Catholic church auditorium in the state of Rhode Island. The church steeple is 185 feet high, and is a thing of beauty. The steeple supports a bell which weighs 2,500 pounds.

The bell is rung regularly on Sundays and special occasions.

The interior of the church is so beautiful that one gets a thrill from the moment he enters. The pews, the rostrum, the clock, the chandelier, the Palladian window and the organ blend together in such symmetry that it seems they belong to each other.

I feel that my scope of knowledge has been increased by my visits to this beautiful and historic church building. (Visit it if you can.)

I conclude my remarks on this church by stating that from what I have seen, also from what I have been able to glean from history, it is my conviction that another church not far distant from this one, has a better claim to being the FIRST BAPTIST CHURCH IN AMERICA.

DR. JOHN CLARKE

This is a photograph of a portrait by the French artist Deville, dated 1659, which hangs in the Redwood Library, New Port, which is assumed to be a likeness of Dr. John Clarke.

THE JOHN CLARKE CHURCH

"John Clarke was born at Westhorpe, Suffolk County, England, October 8, 1609. His father's name was Thomas Clarke. His mother's maiden name was Rose Kerrich. He was one of eight children, six of whom came to America and settled in different parts of New England."

> Quoted from **The Life of John Clarke,** by Rev. Wilbur Nelson

James I sat upon the throne of England 1603-1625. The whole world is without doubt indebted to James I for the popular version of the Bible known as the "Authorized Version" which was published in 1611.

James I was a strong contender for the Divine Right of Kings, and made threats against all who refused to acknowledge his authority, particularly in religious matters. Toward these he was tyrannical. He threatened all nonconformists with these words—"I will either make them conform, or I will harry them out of my kingdom." In this he succeeded, at least in part, for many of his subjects fled the country. Some of these fled to Holland, whence in 1620 a group known as the Pilgrim Fathers came to America aboard the "Mayflower" and settled at Plymouth. Ten years later, even a larger group known as Puritans came from England, settled at Boston, and founded Massachusetts Bay Colony. The Puritans had fled from England rather than conform to the religious whims of a tyrannical king. Without a doubt they sought religious liberty for themselves, but the facts of history prove that they did not grant religious liberty to others. John Clarke was born during the reign of James I, and was among the British subjects which left England because he could not conscientiously conform to the demands of the established church and religion.

In 1636, one Anne Hutchinson, a woman of much intelligence and a good personality, became active in the religious discussions going on in the Massachusetts Bay Colony. She opened a forum for the discussion of civic, social and religious questions in her home about the year 1636. Religiously, she stood for the "Covenant of Faith" as against the "Covenant of Works." She and her followers were called by their opponents "Antinomians." Some of the leading citizens of the colony took her side of the issue, including Harry Vane, who was Governor of the colony. In 1637, John Winthrop, a former governor, won the election over Harry Vane. When Winthrop assumed the office of Governor, the General Court of Massachusetts adopted strenuous measures against the "Antinomians." Some were disfranchised (in order to hold citizenship in the colony, one had to be a member of one of the established churches in the colony), others were banished, and Anne

Hutchinson, their leader, was excommunicated from the church.

While these things were taking place, John Clarke and his wife, Elizabeth, arrived in Boston from England. John Clarke's convictions concerning human liberty were so deeply grounded, that the action taken by the established authorities against Anne Hutchinson and her followers influenced him not to remain in Boston. He allied himself with such people as circumstances compelled to leave Boston and find homes elsewhere.

John Clarke was respected as a man of great learning. He bore high repute for scholarship and ability in languages, including Latin, Greek, Hebrew, and Law, Medicine and Theology. He was by profession a physician and a Baptist minister. He possessed the qualifications of a leader, and a leader he became.

The conditions in Massachusetts Bay Colony became so intolerable in 1637 that John Clarke and some three hundred with him entered into a compact to remove themselves out of the colony. Clarke and some others were chosen to seek out a place for a new colony where liberty of conscience would prevail. Clarke, himself, states that because of the heat in the locality, he thought it advisable to seek a place further North, so they traveled to New Hampshire where they remained for some time, and found the winter so cold that they decided to again go to the South. They had in mind to go to Long Island,

and on returning to the South they came to Providence. They were received by Roger Williams in a very courteous manner, as Williams himself had been a victim of the same conditions that Clarke and his party were leaving in Massachusetts. Through the help received from Roger Williams, and others at Plymouth, they were assured that Aquidneck Island was not in the territory of an established colony, so thither they went to establish a settlement and colony. There were in all about three hundred persons in the group that left Massachusetts with John Clarke. The name of the island was soon changed from Aquidneck to Rhode Island. The land settled by John Clarke and his followers was purchased from the Indians. The date of the transaction was March 24, 1638.

When the group came to a definite decision to leave Boston they drew up and signed the following compact:

> "The seventh day of the first month, 1638.
>
> "We whose names are underwritten do hereby solemnly in the presence of Jehovah incorporate ourselves into a Bodie Politick and, as He shall help, submit our persons, lives and estates unto our Lord Jesus Christ, the King of Kings, and Lord of Lords, and to all those perfect and most absolute laws of His given in His Holy Word of Truth, to be guided and judged thereby."

Exodus 24:3 and 4
I Chron. 11:3
II Kings 11:17

William Coddington,	William Dyre,
John Clarke,	William Freeborne,
William Hutchinson, Jr.,	Philip Shearman,
John Coggeshall,	John Walker,
William Aspinwall,	Richard Carder,
Samuel Wilbore,	William Baulston,
John Sanford,	Edward Hutchinson,
Edward Hutchinson, Jr.,	Sr.,
Esq.,	Henry Bull,
Thomas Savage,	Randall Holden.

It is thought and most generally agreed by historians that John Clarke drew up this compact; William Coddington, whose name appears first, had been chosen President and Judge of the group and it would seem proper that his name head the list. John Clarke's name appears second on the list of signers.

John Clarke and his followers first established a settlement at the north end of the island at a place called by the Indians Pocasset. There were some one hundred families that joined the settlement during the first year. According to Newman's **History of the Baptist Churches in the United States,** the settlement planted by the John Clarke group far outnumbered the Providence settlement and had a much superior government. Quote from Newman's History:

"It should be observed that from the time of the formation of this colony Roger Williams' Providence was still in a rudimentary state, with a population small in comparison with that of the Aquidneck colony, and with scarcely the beginnings of organized political life. The colony under Clarke and Coddington was not only numerically far stronger than that under Williams, but it embraced far more of culture and political experience and wisdom. Portsmouth (the name that replaced Pocasset) [parenthetical statement mine] was the first part of the island to be settled. In April, 1639, Coddington, Clarke, and others organized a new community at Newport. Portsmouth and Newport were reunited in 1640. In 1643, as already stated, Roger Williams was sent to England by the Rhode Island and Providence people conjointly to secure a charter. The charter was secured, but—partly, it may be, on account of the designation 'Providence Plantations,' which may have seemed to give a certain ascendency to Providence—the union of the three settlements under the charter did not take place till 1647."

I now quote a statement from **The Life of Dr. John Clarke,** by Rev. Wilbur Nelson:

"The island which the Indians called 'Aquidneck,' meaning 'Isle of Peace,' was named by the white settlers 'Rhode Island,' and when on March 12, 1640, the towns Portsmouth and Newport united to form a colony they named

their colony 'Rhode Island.' William Coddington was elected governor. Suitable legislation
was enacted, and in March of the following
year, at the General Court of Election, a statute
was adopted which declared the government to
be a 'democracy,' the laws of which it was in
the power of the freemen, by majority vote,
to determine for themselves: 'That none be accounted a delinquent for doctrine'; and that
the official seal should be the figure of a sheaf
of arrows bound together and marked with the
motto—'AMOR VINCET OMNIA.' "

As far as I am able to learn, the above document was the first legislative action for personal,
political and religious liberty on the American
Continent. It may be true that Roger Williams
wrote more on the subject of liberty of conscience
and freedom of man than did John Clarke, but
Clarke did more about it by translating his views
into the statutes of government and into minds
and hearts of men.

John Clarke possessed great powers of discern-
ment, and acted unselfishly in all that he did.
The historical evidence is that he did nothing
with a view of making a name for himself, or of
gracing the pages of history with his deeds. He
labored abundantly for the cause of Baptists in
America, and for the liberties of mankind. He
wanted men to be FREE to vote, to think, to act
and to worship without restraint of church or
government, and in this field he did much in

foundation work relative to our form of free and constitutional government in America.

He had trouble with what appeared to be the designs of selfish men, but in these disappointments, he showed himself a man of self-mastery and ability to meet the situations and overcome them for the good of all.

The evidence is that almost from the beginning there was rivalry between Providence (Roger Williams' settlement) and Rhode Island (John Clarke's settlement) both in political and religious matters. Quoting again from the **Life of Dr. John Clarke,** by Rev. Wilbur Nelson:

> "In the meantime the towns of Providence and Warwick were growing up, and Roger Williams made a trip to England and secured a charter incorporating Providence, Warwick, Newport and Portsmouth into a colony to be known as 'The Colony of Providence Plantations in the Narragansett Bay in New England.' He returned home with his charter in 1643. Williams, however, had not been commisisoned by the residents of Newport and Portsmouth to secure such a charter, and it was not until four years later that they were satisfied to adopt it. Finally, however, in 1647 all four towns accepted the charter, and John Coggeshall became the first president of the new colony.

> "To the charter was appended a code of laws, in the preamble of which it was declared that

'the form of government established in Providence Plantations is Democratical, held by free and voluntary consent of all, or the greater part, of the free inhabitants,' and it was further guaranteed that all should enjoy in peace and quiet their rights and liberties. Dr. Clarke appears to have been recognized as a legal authority, and he is supposed to have been the author of this remarkable code, concerning which Gov. Arnold in his 'History of Rhode Island' has written: 'We hazard little in saying that the digest of 1647, for simplicity of diction, unencumbered as it is by the superfluous verbiage that clothes our modern statutes in learned obscurity; for breadth of comprehension, embracing as it does the foundation for the whole body of law, on every subject, which has since been adopted; and for vigor, and originality of thought, and boldness of expression, as well as for the vast significance and the brilliant triumph of the principles it embodies, presents a model of legislation which has never been surpassed!'"

So it is, that, John Clarke took the unrequested charter secured by Roger Williams and amplified it in a way to distinguish himself as a legal authority and a lover of the liberties of men; also, to change the charter in a manner to make it acceptable to the colony.

In 1649 Charles the I of England was executed, and a popular form of government known as the "Commonwealth of England" was set up with

Oliver Cromwell as Head of the Council of State. Under the advantages of the changed conditions in England, William Coddington, who had been for several years associated with Clarke, and who had been honored with the office of president of the colony, had personal political ambitions and secretly made a trip to England and obtained a commission which virtually annulled the charter by separating the towns of Newport and Portsmouth from Providence and Warwick and making him governor for life of the Islands of Aquidneck and Conanicut, a position of virtual sovereignty. This act of William Coddington so aroused the entire colony that in 1651 Dr. Clarke and Roger Williams were sent to England to get his commission revoked. With the assistance of Sir Harry Vane and John Milton they were successful in their effort to get Coddington's commission revoked. After this Williams returned home, but Dr. Clarke remained in England to safeguard the interests of the colony. It was twelve years before he returned home.

The position held and the responsibilities borne by Dr. Clarke during this long stay in England were difficult and trying. I quote a statement from Dr. Barrows:

"To appreciate his labors as agent, we must know the obstacles he had to overcome, in the prosecution of his mission. His post was one of exceeding difficulty. He represented a state anomalous in the history of the world. Her principles were deemed subversive of order and good government, and destructive to religion. Her democracy was offensive to the colonies about her. Hence their efforts to annoy her, to foment dissensions within her territory, to annihilate the little state, whose principles they could not understand. . . . The principles of Rhode Island were not only caricatured by enemies, but often ignorantly defended by friends. The very freedom permitted in the colony brought to it many restless spirits who could live peaceably nowhere else, and jealousy for their liberties not frequently led to troubles. These dissensions, sometimes indeed exceedingly bitter, tended to bring into disrepute the government which Dr. Clarke was expected to vindicate before its enemies. . . . Yet through al these difficulties he steered his way with a steady hand. He preserved his colony from loss, enlarged her boundaries, and secured for her a more stable government, while resorting to no dishonorable means, but maintaining his integrity."

In the enlargement of the territory of the colony Dr. Clarke gained territory that was held in dispute between his colony and that of both Massachusetts and Connecticut. These two colonies were chagrined by Dr. Clarke's success, and it would be natural for them to insinuate Dr. Clarke employed unfair tactics to gain his point, but he is vindicated by the history of the time, while it reflects gravely upon the methods of his traducers.

Soon after Charles II came to the throne of England in 1660, the charter secured by Roger Williams was annulled, and it became necessary that a new charter be secured immediately. The securing of this charter was the task and responsibility of Dr. Clarke. The charter secured by Williams did not recognize Rhode Island in its title. Its title was as follows: "The Colony of Providence Plantations in the Narragansett Bay in New England." This was the charter that was revoked.

In presenting the labors of Dr. Clarke in securing the new charter from Charles II, I think the historic narrative given by Rev. Wilbur Nelson in his booklet, **The Life of Dr. John Clarke,** is the best that I have read, and from it I quote as follows:

"It was a time when a great statesman and diplomat was needed. Fortunately such a man, in the person of Dr. John Clarke, was at hand. Man of ability and scholarship that he was, he wrote the charter himself, thus incorporating into it all that was desired, and, then with a diplomacy that has never been excelled, if even equaled, in the face of bitter opposition and personal abuse, he secured the signature and seal of King Charles II on July 8, 1663.

"Under this charter the colony now became known as 'The Colony of Rhode Island of 1663,' says Dr. Bicknell, 'has been universally recognized as the most liberal state paper ever

issued by the English Crown.' In it absolute
religious freedom was for the first time in the
history of the world secured and guaranteed.
It was so democratic, both in letter and spirit,
that doubts were entertained in England
whether the king had a right to grant it. It
was so broad, so practical, so efficient in its
provisions that it continued in force until the
colony became a state, and then continued as
the constitution of the 'State of Rhode Island
and Providence Plantations' for sixty - seven
years, until in 1843 the present state constitution was adopted. But the principles it embodied still live, not only in the constitution
and laws of Rhode Island but in the government of every state in the union, and they are
making their way into other countries and
becoming the principles of government of the
world.

"In his petition to the King as in the charter
itself, Dr. Clarke used the following words,
which have been inscribed as an imperishable
sentiment on the West Facade of the Capitol
in Providence — 'THAT IT IS MUCH ON
THEIR HEARTS (IF THEY MAY BE PER-
MITTED) TO HOLD FORTH A LIVELY
EXPERIMENT, THAT A MOST FLOURISH-
ING CIVIL STATE MAY STAND AND BEST
BE MAINTAINED, AND THAT AMONG OUR
ENGLISH SUBJECTS, WITH A FULL LIB-
ERTY IN RELIGIOUS CONCERNMENTS.'"

The contents of the charter written and secured
by Dr. John Clarke met with much favorable

comment, and now I offer a few statements made by prominent men, and in giving these I quote further from Rev. Nelson:

> "Honorable John R. Bartlett, former Secretary of State for Rhode Island, has said: 'Rhode Island owes to John Clarke a monument of granite and a statue of bronze.' John Callandar declared: 'His memory is deserving of lasting honor for his efforts toward establishing the first government in the world, which gave all equal civil and religious liberty.' Thomas W. Bicknell has written: 'Had Dr. John Clarke of Newport no other claim to the first place among the founders of the American Colonies, the Royal Charter of 1663 would confer that honor.' "

It is very gratifying to know that a Baptist minister of the gospel of Jesus Christ became both the author and obtainer of the first legal state document in the world that guaranteed civil and religious liberty to all its subjects. (I am proud to be a Baptist minister, and to believe in the doctrines and principles of Dr. John Clarke.)

Dr. Clarke proved his unselfish devotion to the causes that he represented during his long stay in England by supporting himself, and in order to do so he was forced to mortgage his holdings in the colony.

The best reaction of the people of the colony to the success of Dr. Clarke's mission to England that I have read is the account given by Newman in his **A History of the Baptist Churches in the United States** on page 107:

> "There was universal rejoicing throughout Rhode Island and Providence Plantations that the aspirations of the colonists for liberty and for their rights in relation to the other colonies had been so amply secured by their honored and beloved agent. The bearer of the royally sealed document was handsomely rewarded for his fidelity. It was voted 'that Mr. John Clarke, the colony's agent in England, be saved harmless in his estate; and to that end that all his disbursements going to England, and all his expenses and engagements there already laid out . . . as also . . . expenses and engagements he shall be necessitated yet further to imburse . . . shall be repaid, paid, and discharged by this Colony. . . . That in consideration of . . . his great pains, labor and travail with much faithfulness exercised for above twelve years in behalf of this Colony, in England, the thanks of the Colony be sent unto him by the Governor and Deputy Governor; and for a gratuity unto him, the Assembly engage that the Colony shall pay unto the said John Clarke . . . over and besides what is above engaged, the sum . . . of one hundred pounds sterling.' "

After Dr. Clarke's return to the colony, he resumed his practice of medicine and the pastorate of the church he had established, in which capacities he served until his death in April, 1676.

He also held the public offices of deputy assemblyman, and deputy governor.

The Medical Society of Newport honored Dr. Clarke as a member of their profession by placing on the walls of the Newport Historical Society a tablet with the following inscription:

ERECTED BY THE NEWPORT MEDICAL
SOCIETY,

DECEMBER 1885

TO

JOHN CLARKE, PHYSICIAN
1609-1676

FOUNDER OF NEWPORT
AND OF THE CIVIL POLITY OF
RHODE ISLAND

In the last will and testament of Dr. John Clarke, he showed his interest in education by setting up a trust supported by some of his property, to be administered by three trustees and their successors for the purpose of "bringing up children unto learning, and for the relief of the poor." This is believed to be the oldest active trust in the United States.

In recognition of Dr. Clarke's notable services as a statesman and scholar, Rhode Island College in Providence dedicated its new John Clarke

Science Building in 1963. This was the first state-owned building to bear his name. One of the grammar schools of Newport is named for him.

Quoting again from Rev. Nelson:

"One historian says, 'He was one of the most eminent men of the seventeenth century.' Another declares that 'for many years before his death he was the most important man in his colony.' Still another says: 'No character in New England is of purer fame than John Clarke.' He was in every way worthy of the movement that has been started to enroll his name in the National Hall of Fame."

THE UNITED BAPTIST CHURCH

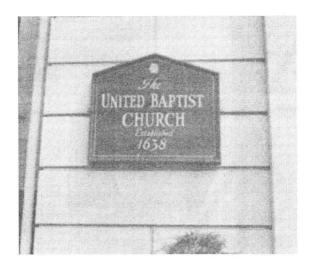

I close this brief history by making a few statements on the name of the church in Newport, Rhode Island.

There are historic statements which lead me to believe that John Clarke began his ministry with the people of his colony immediately after they settled at the north end of Aquidneck Island, first called by its Indian name, Pocasset, and in 1638 changed to Portsmouth, and a meeting house built. Then during the next year in April, 1639, Dr. Clarke and others moved to the present site of the city of Newport and founded Newport where another meeting house was erected. It is believed by historians that the church begun at Portsmouth in 1638 was moved along with the settlers to Newport, where it has continued in active service ever since, with the exception of a period of interruption during the Revolutionary War when the British occupied the town of Newport. As far as I am able to learn from the material at hand, the following from the program of the 325th Anniversary Service is the best and most authentic data on the name of the church:

> "The United Baptist Church, John Clarke Memorial, takes its name from a reunion of the First Baptist Church John Clarke Memorial and the Second Baptist Church which was brought about in 1946, after nearly three hundred years of separation. That separation took place in 1656, when twenty-one members with-

drew from the First Church and formed a Six Principle Baptist Church.

"In 1847 some sixty members withdrew from the Second Baptist Church and formed the Central Baptist Church. Those two churches were reunited in 1906 under the name of the Second Baptist Church. So the United Baptist Church is really a merger of the First, Second, and Central Baptist Churches of Newport. . . .

"The old First Baptist meeting-house, now the home of the United Baptist Church, was originally dedicated in 1846. It stands on the site of a previous meeting-house built in 1738."

The First Baptist Church, John Clarke Memorial, is affiliated with the American Baptist Convention at the present time.*

While in the church building and in conversation with Mrs. Mary K. Doolittle, secretary to the pastor, Rev. L. Edgar Stone, Jr., I asked if the church was segregated or integrated in its membership, and was told that its membership was all white. This was in the year 1964.

In this effort, I have tried to avoid repetition of what is so clearly set forth in the book to which my brief history is but an appendage, such as the persecution of Clarke, Holmes, and Crandall.

I shall always be glad that I had the privilege of visiting this historic church, and to stand in the cemetery where the remains of John Clarke rest in peace till the dawn of the Resurrection Morning, when, at the sound of the trumpet of God, he shall be raised to the glorious immortality that his faith in the Lord Jesus Christ vouchsafes unto him.

While standing by his grave, I thought of Moses standing before the burning bush, and could sense that I was standing on Holy Ground.

I assure the reader of this statement, that it

---

* I drew a wrong conclusion from the name of the church, and once made a public statement that the church was of the order of the "United Baptists of Kentucky"; in this I was in error.

has been a pleasure to me to prepare this document, and I submit it for publication in the hope that all statements are accurate, and that just honors have been paid to the great men, whose names appear in it.

BIBLIOGRAPHY

The First Baptist Church in America Not Founded by Roger Williams, Graves & Adlam.

History of the Baptists, Backus, Vol. I.

History of the Baptists in the United States, Newman.

History of the Baptists in New England, Burrage.

The Life of Dr. John Clarke, Rev. Wilbur Nelson.

Historical Sketch and Directory of Historical Room, United Baptist Church.

325th Anniversary Service of The United Baptist Church John Clarke Memorial, Anniversary Committee: Wilbur Nelson, Louis Young, Mrs. Alfred Mikkelson, William Hope, and Rev. L. Edgar Stone, Jr.

The First Baptist Church, Providence, Rhode Island, Rev. Henry M. King, D.D.

Brochure — "The First Baptist Church in America, Providence, Rhode Island."

The pictures are taken from the brochures, books, and leaflets secured in the churches, as well as pictures made by my family while there.